Also from Clevedon Community Press

Writing on the Lake: an anthology of poetry and prose, 2016
ISBN: 978-0-9935666-0-8

Jane Lilly
Clevedon Cuttings: history, houses and a couple of characters,
2017
ISBN: 978-0-9935666-1-5

John Birkinshaw
Celebrating Portishead Open Air Pool, 2018
ISBN: 978-0-99356666-2-2

In the Footsteps of Poets: inspired by Clevedon, 2019
ISBN: 978-0-9935666-3-9

FARMS, FOLK and FAMOUS PEOPLE

Histories of Clevedon

ABOUT THE AUTHOR

Jane Lilly was born in The Knoll Nursing Home many years ago and has never lived outside Clevedon. She has been researching the history of Clevedon since 1974 and probably will never find out everything she would like to know. She is not discouraged by this. The first of her many local history books was published in 1990, after she had already contributed essays on local topics to books published by Clevedon Civic Society Local History Group. Jane is now an Honorary Member of Clevedon Archaeological Society. She provided the information and images for the local history displays in the visitor centre on Clevedon Pier, Discover@The Pier. Jane is of the firm opinion that Clevedon is the best place in the known universe. This is Jane's second book published by Clevedon Community Press.

FARMS, FOLK and FAMOUS PEOPLE

Histories of Clevedon

[signature]

Jane Lilly

with a memoir by Derek B Lilly

Clevedon Community Press

ISBN: 978-0-9935666-4-6

First published 2020 by
Clevedon Community Press
Unit 15, Tweed Road Estate
Clevedon BS21 6RR

Author: Jane Lilly
Cover design and illustrator: Stephanie Fitch
Copy editor: Guy Johnson
Printed and bound by: bookprintinguk

Dedication

With many belated and heartfelt thanks to the Pier Supporters Club, for their determination and hard work in keeping the Clevedon Pier standing from the time it collapsed in 1970 until it could be saved ten years later.

Without their determined efforts, the pier would have been demolished, the seafront would look very bare and, without the pier, Clevedon's seafront would lose a large part of its character.

Acknowledgements

As ever, Derek Lilly and David Long have been very generous with their photographs. Tom Lilly, Derek's oldest brother, handed on to us his own collection, photographs taken in the late 1920s and early 1930s.

I've also had help with illustrations from Veronica Wainwright and Barbara Connell. Information about the Fishley Holland Pottery came from the late Bill Holland and the late George Holland.

The knowledge and expertise of the Somerset Vernacular Buildings Research Group has been invaluable, along with permission from the Pearce family and the Kirk family for access to their houses.

Lily Style was a great help with family photographs and detail for the Nelson essay, for which she allowed me use of photographs owned by the Style and Tribe families. I would thoroughly recommend her website on the Nelson family and their associations: http://lilystyle.co.uk/blanckleys-1832-64.html

The late Rob Campbell made sure that I was able to have Ted Caple's albums, a generous gift from the late Bill Griffin. Rob, we all miss you!

A very useful book I found in Clevedon Library would be interesting to most Clevedonians: *A Sweet family of Yatton, Kingston Seymour and Clevedon, North Somerset*, by Josephine White, no date. It was a great help with Dowlais Farm.

Many years ago now I wrote to both Jan and Gareth Morris asking them if they would write for me short reminiscences about their childhood memories of Clevedon, which they kindly did.

David Sutcliffe was kind enough to read the chapter, Song and Dance and Clevedon, and put me right on several points. His own book on Charles Marson is excellent. I heartily recommend it.

My grateful thanks, as ever, to MS whose proof–reading skills and vocabulary improve my work.

Jane Lilly   September 2019

Contents

Illustrations

Introduction

Some topics in this collection have been simmering on a back burner for a long time. Some, particularly the Clevedon Pottery, have featured in previous publications.

In 2019, it was fifty years since William Fishley Holland died a remarkable craftsman and character here in Clevedon. I have written about his pottery in a booklet published by Weston Museum some 25 years ago, as well as in Clevedon Civic Society's book, *Clevedon's Social and Industrial Heritage*, but somehow there is always more to say.

Lake Farm is one of the most interesting farm houses I have visited locally, along with Dowlais Farm and, above all, Highdale Farm.

Many famous people have associations with our town, enough for a book of their own, but Nelson is one of my own heroes and his family's connection with Clevedon is little known.

It was surprising to discover over a span of many years that several of our most notable folk song collectors have been associated with Clevedon, as well as many ordinary people who revived Morris Dancing here in 1908 during the early years of the renaissance of this dance form.

Mr Fowler was notable in erecting the first purpose-built shop here as the town began to grow in the late 1820s, an elegant long-surviving triumph. The extent of the development on his large plot of ground at the seaward end of Hill Road is surprising.

The Lawn School was the most select of the many small boarding schools for young ladies in Clevedon – and there were many. The healthy atmosphere here was very popular with the middle classes and those who served in tropical climes as well. As Derek Lilly says, Clevedon suited their budgets.

The Morris family shouldn't need an introduction, but I will just say that they are remarkable. Their connection with Clevedon has brought us much credit and should be more widely known.

Finally, I have included a short reminiscence written by Derek Lilly, my uncle, who is an untidy reprobate much loved by his family. It's from a different age – you'll enjoy it!

Chapter 1

Clevedon Pottery: William Fishley Holland

The old Clevedon Pottery, situated in Court Lane, was sold by the Holland family in 1977. This is a turning to the right just before you reach Clevedon Court when going out of Clevedon. It was in the first buildings on the right hand side of the lane, which now form part of a complex of holiday cottages.

William Fishley Holland was born in Fremington, near Barnstaple, in 1889, where his father was a farmer. His mother, Isabel, was the daughter of Edwin Beer Fishley, one of a line of noted peasant potters established at Fremington in North Devon since 1800. They worked the clays from the Yelland clay seam which produced excellent earthenware.

William became a potter himself when his widowed mother returned to Fremington in 1902 to nurse her own mother. He spent the next ten years at the pottery there with his grandfather, who owned the pottery, learning to make the workaday pots still in demand at that time: flowerpots, bread crocks, baking dishes, baking pans, colanders, animal feed troughs – the list was almost endless. The pottery at Fremington was well known in Cornwall for making the best salting vessels for pilchards. One of their employees was the last man to make the thick-walled cloam ovens to be used in a fireplace for making bread and other baked goods. Some ornamental wares were also popular, and the harvest jugs made by William's forebears, decorated with traditional rhymes, are collected avidly today.

In 1910, William married Annie Jane Richards and they started a family. Constance Mary Holland was born in 1910, followed by George Tonkin Holland in 1912, Isabel Annie Holland in 1914, finishing neatly in 1915 with William Fishley Holland, known as Bill.

Plate 1: William Fishley Holland at work in the 1950s

Sadly, after William's grandfather's death in 1912, the pottery was sold and the money divided between his mother and her siblings.

William found a job for himself organising the foundation of a new pottery at Braunton owned by a Mr Hooper, a local solicitor. Bankruptcy caused the sale of that pottery in 1921. There was some chicanery with regard to the sale and William, though he had hoped to take the pottery himself, declined to buy the business.

At this point, two opportunities arose. William could have gone to work with Bernard Leach, who was setting up his famous pottery at St Ives in Cornwall. However, he decided that he would prefer to work independently and took a job in Clevedon. Sir Edmund Elton had died the previous year and his son, Sir Ambrose, needed a potter to throw 'blanks' to be decorated with the Eltonware glazes that his father had made famous from the 1880s onwards.

Eltonware was an Art pottery, a different style from that to which William was accustomed. He was only required to work a day or so a week making the blanks, and the rest of the time was his own. He was to have the use of the pottery workshop in Clevedon Court.

By now, the children were all of school age so he chose to move to Clevedon where good schooling would be far easier to find for them. After about a year, Art pottery faded from popularity and Bernard Leach's style of Studio pottery became by far the most favoured fashion.

In 1922, William bought a house with a little land in Court Lane, Clevedon, for £475 and made improvements to the 17th century building. The garden was soon put into productive and tidy order. A new notice saying 'Inspection invited' placed next to the sign for his new 'Clevedon Pottery' soon brought visitors and customers along. Coach parties, which were beginning to tour the area, called on the Pottery, which proved to be a very popular destination.

With William came George Manley, a young man he had trained at Braunton. The two men were very lively and outgoing, which helped to attract visitors.

William erected his own brick-built kiln shaped like a large bottle which was eventually replaced in the early 1950s with an electric kiln. Legend has it that it was at this point, while his father was away, that George borrowed a bulldozer and knocked the old kiln down to make way for a new building! By that time, George, having served in the Royal Navy during the War, had become his own man. He had learned potting under his father's excellent tuition.

The items made at Clevedon Pottery were smaller than the Devon wares that William had grown up with. As he had done at Braunton, he introduced brightly coloured glazes and attractive domestic pieces, jugs, tankards and beakers, all largely for use at the table rather than in the kitchen.

Plate 2: George Manley putting handles on jugs

The range of colours produced before the Second World War was quite something: buttercup yellow, pale blue, deep cobalt blue, pink, black, brown, mustard yellow, orange, dark red, pale green, emerald green and buff. The orange in particular was much prized. Several other potters tried to emulate the quality of the colour, but failed.

From the 1950s onwards, the colours changed to become paler, grey, light green, a light turquoise, cream and brown. This was due to the use of different glazes. I am told that the old glazes used lead which, by that time, was thought not to be safe to use. The orange glaze, in fact, contained uranium, far more dangerous than lead! By then, slip decoration had been introduced for the pots, much improved by Bill Janes, who worked at the Pottery after the War.

At Braunton, William had taught the young Michael Cardew to throw pottery on the wheel. Cardew became Bernard Leach's first student, later an exceptionally able potter in his own right. Both Leach and Cardew visited the Clevedon Pottery at Court Lane and enjoyed exchanging news with William as they watched him at work.

William was firmly embedded in the local community, having joined the East Clevedon Debating Society. He became a town councillor as well as sitting on the Carnival Committee, Flower Show Committee and the Ratepayers' Association. He helped to form an Unemployment Committee during the Great Depression which raised funds in order to provide work for the unemployed men in the town. One of these projects was the laying out of the footpath around Wain's Hill and Old Church Hill known as Poets' Walk. Men were also employed on the building of the Marine Lake.

George Tonkin Holland took part in local amateur dramatics, undertaking stage management and production and even cutting out the costumes when needed!

In 1948, William made a copy of one of his feathered bowls which Queen Elizabeth, later the Queen Mother, had seen and admired. The purchaser had offered it to her as a gift, but William offered to make one for her. The letter of thanks for the gift was a great prize, and the words 'Patronised by H M Queen Elizabeth' were added to the Pottery's advertisements in local guide books thereafter.

School groups visited the Pottery. At one point, having said he could probably make a pot with his eyes shut, William had to show that he could! The children carefully blindfolded him and watched as the pot rose from the lump of clay on the wheel. The pot had 'Pot made by Mr Holland with his eyes shut' inscribed on the base and was kept by the headmaster's wife as a prized possession.

Older examples and replicas of the Fishley Pottery were proudly displayed in part of the showroom, used as a museum, some dating right back to the early 19th century when George Fishley first founded the family business.

Of the four Holland children, two worked at the Clevedon Pottery. Isabel made delightful figurines as well as throwing at the wheel. George, the oldest, was exceptionally gifted. He moved to Dunster in 1958 to run his own pottery for seven years, then taught at Minehead Further Education Centre before retiring. He was fiercely proud of being born at Fremington and of being a fifth–generation potter. (George and Constance Holland were born at Fremington, Isabel and Bill probably at Braunton, also in North Devon: the births were registered in Barnstaple.)

After George had left, William stayed at the Pottery. In 1958, he had his autobiography published in the *Pottery Quarterly Journal*, telling the vivid story of his life as a potter. This book is now a collectors' item detailing, as it does, the work that went into setting up potteries, working at various trade fairs around the country, and life as one of the last of a generation of true country potters. William's wife Annie died in 1959 and, when he remarried, he moved out of the house in Court Lane.

For a couple of years, William's grandson St John Child, his older daughter's son, ran the Pottery, but left to train as an artist. Bill Holland, his younger son, who had trained and worked as an architect, moved to the Pottery and managed the business from 1960 until it closed in 1977.

For a short time after that, a keen stoneware potter called Norman Darby worked from the old Clevedon Pottery. To his horror, he discovered that the name had never been registered, so promptly rectified this! Sadly, he developed arthritis and had to give up the Pottery. For a number of years, it was a small craft centre.

Before William died in 1969 he saw his grandson Peter become a potter in his turn.

In 2019, we celebrate 130 years since William Fishley Holland's birth, as well as 50 years since his death.

To end, I can't better his own final words from *Fifty Years a Potter*:

> Mine has been a happy life, not without its ups and downs, as is the lot of most men. It matters a great deal what you wish to bring into your life. I would say that you can attract good if you desire it and that evil will come only if you make no effort to keep it away. Happiness comes by helping in any good work and with it comes peace of mind.

Chapter 2

Lake Farm, once Cole House

Lake Farm is at the end of a bumpy track off the south side of Colehouse Lane and lies just within Kenn. It is a long, three storey building now divided into three dwellings, once upon a time thatched, now tiled.

Plate 3: Lake Farm following restoration in 2005

The house was originally called Cole House and was the main home of the Cole Family at the heart of whose small estate it stood, possibly their Manor House. The fact that their largest nearby farm was called Cole House Farm became a source of confusion and, in the last century, Cole House became Lake Farm, leaving the farm to carry the name exclusively.

The family after whom the house is named is deeply rooted in Kenn and the neighbouring village of Kingston Seymour. Their surname is Saxon and means 'swarthy in colouring'. Although the house is in Kenn, the lands and farmhouses which formed the rest of the Cole Estate lie largely within the Clevedon parish boundary. The fact that the land they held straddles the parish boundaries of Kenn and Clevedon could indicate that it was held as a Manor in Saxon times – but we have no evidence.

As early as 1242, Richard Cole and his brother, Walter of Kingston Seymour, together with Thomas de Marisco, were accused of beating and wounding Nicholas Thorel of the same place. The judges found the Coles guilty and kept them in custody. William Cole, possibly their father, was made to pledge five marks of the whole of his tithing at Kingston [there were three marks to the pound]. This was a substantial amount of money and a serious fine.

The family appears again in 1321 in one of the surviving Manorial Rolls for Clevedon. This Roll deals with crimes and misdemeanors and records that:

> John Cole has long owed ditching between the road towards Oldevelde and his demesne land. He is seized of the ditches on both sides of the aforesaid road; ground of the lord of Clevedon and which pertains to him.

He should have been keeping the ditches clear: in low-lying ground the drainage was crucial to the success or failure of crops, and flooding could endanger grazing land. The field in question lay north-west of the house, reached by Colehouse Lane itself. The ditches that still lie along the sides of Colehouse Lane are the ditches his workers should have been keeping clear.

When the Exchequer Lay Subsidy was collected in 1326, there were another two members of the Cole family making payments. In Kingston Seymour, Juliana Cole paid 21 shillings, and in Kenn, Willelmo Cole paid 6d – evidently his landholding was smaller than hers. This was a tax paid on movable possessions, usually at one fifteenth of their value for country dwellers.

In another of the surviving Rolls for Clevedon Manor, a Rental of 1388/9, keeping track of tenants and their duties in return for their landholding, John Cole has rights over a lane called Briddeswey. He paid 6d for that lane and handed over a capon for the feast of St Martin (11 November). He also had to spend a day weeding for the Lord of the Manor at Clevedon. [Roll 7660 1388/9, British Museum.]

For several centuries, no records seem to survive regarding Cole House. The thread is picked up again in 1578 when John Apery, or Perry, took possession of a garden plot. This was quoted in a document used later to prove the right of the owner to sell the land. The garden plot was described as being

> ...ditched and bounded round about with quick sett and with great trees of elme in the utter (outer) bounds thereof containing by estimation 8 & 20 yards square.... lying and being in Kenne, with and within the same garden and within a yard of the utter [outer] bounds of the same.... planted with quick sett [fast growing small bushes which would have been kept trimmed to a rounded shape] to hang and dry cloathes on and lying and adjoining within 9 yards on and adjoining to the west parte and end of the kitchen coyninge [corner] of the then dwelling house and Court of said John Aperry sometimes called Cole House in Kenne....

By 1578, when he took possession of this drying ground, he already had Cole House itself.

By 1616/7, the house and land was owned by John Aperry's

son, Christopher Perry. He and his wife (née Coules) levied a fine on Cole House for an annuity for themselves. The annuity was to pass next to Richard Newman and his wife, Christopher Perry's daughter Elizabeth, and the heirs of her body. The house was promised to the right heirs of Christopher Perry, presumably to go to them if Elizabeth produced no children of her own.

The next document dates from 1648 when Richard Newman the Elder settled Cole House on his son, Richard Newman the Younger, son of his wife Elizabeth, née Perry. Richard the Elder had the house for his life, then to be passed to his son Richard, and then to Anne Harbord, his son's wife. After that, it was to go to the heirs of the body of Richard Newman the Younger and his wife, or for want of children, to his right heirs. (Anne Harbord, incidentally, was the daughter of Sir Charles Harbord, owner of a substantial estate in Hertfordshire, Moore Park, near Rickmansworth.) In this document of 1648, a dovehouse was listed as part of the property at Cole House. These were substantial buildings, in themselves a badge of the owner's rank, and would certainly indicate a house of considerable status. In early times they were only allowed to be owned or built by the upper echelons of society.

In 1653, Richard Newman the Elder, Richard Newman the Younger and Anne Newman leased the house to John Willoughby of Bristol. Mr Willoughby was a member of the Clockmakers' Company and a grandson of John Willoughby of Beverstock in Wiltshire. He was Mayor of Bristol in 1655 and had married Mary, the daughter of Richard Aldworth of that city, who had been an alderman and Mayor also. Incidentally, Richard's father Robert and his wife Martha feature on a fine monument in St Peter's Church in Bristol.

An undated document of approximately 1660 is an account of rents for the estate Mr Willoughby owned. This refers to Cole House Farm, Late Richard Preston's Tenement, Plomer's 9 Acres, the Tiled House and land, Joseph Horte's Tenement, Stephen Blackmore's Tenement and Mr Pomroy's. This is confusing, but

Lake Farm at this date is Cole House. The Tiled House is what we now know as Cole House Farm. Evidence for this comes from the Clevedon Estate Map of 1853 shown to me by Margaret, Lady Elton some years ago. I copied farm names given on that map: our present-day Cole House Farm was called, 'Knight's Tiled Farm House'.

John Willoughby only used part of Cole House. In 1666, he leased it with all appurtenances to John Young of Hewish. Reserved for Willoughby's use, are

> ...the little chamber over the buttery or cellar and the cockloft over it, with ingress and egress to and from the said premises at all times, except likewise the use in common with John Young of the kitchen in the dwelling house and the kitchen in the outhouse as often as John Willoughby shall have occasion to use the same for washing, brewing, baking or dressing provisions.

John Young would have been the tenant and Mr Willoughby's servants occasionally visited the house and would have had the use of the areas reserved for them.

In 1669, John Willoughby settled Cole House and all his other property on his wife Martha Aldwarth, or Aldworth. It is described as

> A capital messuage or tenement in Kenn, Cole House, and two acres in Clevedon, called Freeland, on the west side of the messuage or tenement, and half an acre in Dugnam in Clevedon. [Dugnam was a large complex of arable fields in the lower part of Strode Road in Clevedon.] It was heretofore the inheritance of Christopher Perry.

By 1700, Cole House was in the hands of Benjamin Willoughby, John's son. Benjamin was a noted clockmaker trained in London by Robert Dingley. He worked from Small Street in Bristol until 1710 and died in Bristol in 1725. It was often the case that men who made their fortune in cities like Bristol invested in farmland in nearby settlements. Farming methods had been much improved by this time and there was a lot of money to be made.

In 1745, Benjamin Willoughby's son, Christopher, has possession of Cole House. The house had formerly been occupied by John Preston and, most recently, by William Sperring. In 1745, it was let to Edward Gwatkin. The house came with a mere two-and-a-half acres so presumably it was a dwelling rather than a farm house. It's possible, though, that Mr Gwatkin leased more land to supplement his income.

The Land Tax assessment of 1759 shows the total value of Willoughby's holdings at some £200 a year, a very considerable income. The tax was paid at 5% of this amount in total, on Cole House, Cole House Farm, Plummer's farm in Kenn Road and on two farms along the Kenn Yeo called Pomroy's and Preston's.

Later Land Tax entries are also helpful, showing that Christopher Willoughby occupied the house until 1768 when it was leased to Nicholas Stock. The Willoughby family still owned the house in December 1798 when the Land Tax was paid by Nicholas Stock at £4/11/0d a year.

Nicholas Stock and his wife Joan had four children christened at St Andrew's Church in Clevedon between 1797 and 1805. Several of the children would have been born after they left Cole House because, in 1800, Nicholas Stock, described as a gentleman of Kenn, bought a lease on a small house in Clevedon from William Long. Seven years later, the lease was sold again and I assume that the Stock family had moved on. The house is number 5 East Clevedon Triangle, built originally in 1798, the first house to be built there. By 1802, the Rates show that Nicholas Stock was renting a smallholding from the Clevedon Court Estate called

Barber's.

The owner by this time was William Coombes who farmed Cole House himself for a few years. After a gap in the surviving records, the Tithe Award lists Edward Holder as the lessee in 1841, with Messrs Lyddon Esquires the owners. The land covered 63 acres 3 roods and 19 perches rented for £122/17/7d. Further land, part of Cole House, was rented by John Griffin from a different owner, Nicholas Jersey Lovell. He was a surgeon from the parish of St George, Somerset. The Rates for Kenn in 1840 record that Mr Holder also rented additional land from Thomas Coombes who held the part of Cole House that lay in Clevedon.

Edward Holder and his wife Harriet lived at the house with their children, including their son Edward and his wife Frances, with their little boy, three year old Edward. Three Edwards in the same house must have occasionally given rise to confusion! The younger Edward moved to Kenn Street a few years later and set himself up selling cider.

The census of 1851 shows that William Butt from Winford was at Cole House for a while farming 80 acres with the help of three hired labourers. Two of the labourers lived in the house with the family which, at that point, consisted of William's wife Patience, their two young children, Benjamin and Charles, aged three and two, as well as his wife's sister, Sarah Poll.

Ten years afterwards, William Butt had moved back to Winford, Cole House being occupied by John Board who came from Berrow near Weston-super-Mare. He and his wife were childless and the 1871 census shows that he employed two men. His ten-year-old nephew and a dairymaid lived in the house with the family.

John Board stayed until his death in 1879. The 1871 census lists the household as consisting of himself and his wife Sarah, three of his nieces staying as visitors and a farm servant, Eleanor Walton. He farmed 79 acres with two men and a boy to help.

While Mr Board had Cole House, Henry Withey from

Dundry was farming at Cole House Farm. He evidently had his eye on Cole House because, in 1880, when Mr Board's possessions and stock were advertised for sale, Cole House Farm was also being cleared, Mr Withey having taken another farm.

Mr Board's effects were auctioned in August and September 1880. The August sale disposed of the farm stock, including 16 prime dairy cows in milk, eight heifers, a bull, seven calves, a cart mare, a bay pony and a hackney horse, good in saddle and harness; four fat pigs and a sow in farrow; 30 tons of English hay, six tons of clover hay, four tons of wheat straw, 70 acres of grass in lots, four acres of clover to be mown and the hay removed. The apples were from about four acres of orchards.

This first sale also included the implements, a wagon, a putt, a cart, a haymaking machine, chain harrow, turnip cutter, sheep rack, hay collector, wheelbarrow, hay knives, field roller and so forth.

In the second sale in September, the goods paint a fascinating picture of the interior of the house. There were four-post and tent beds, chests of drawers and washstands with their basins and jugs, dressing tables, towel racks, mahogany and pine tables, and a wide range of chairs, sofas and carpets. And there were fenders and fire irons, a barometer, a washing machine, a safe, an American cooking stove, a settle, a great amount of kitchen paraphernalia and kettles as well as cooking pots and a bacon rack.

Also sold were the dairy implements, cheese press, churns, milk coolers and vats. From outdoors, a double-roll apple mill, double-screw cider press, hair cloths, casks of several sizes, chaff machine, pig troughs, harness, a winnowing machine and even cucumber lights figured among the many items for sale.

Henry Withey's family settled comfortably at Cole House, with a man to assist Henry as he farmed the 80 acres of land that came with it. His son William, aged 19, helped also. His daughter was 21 and would have been expected to help her mother, probably also doing dairy work, which usually fell to the women on a farm.

Henry died in 1883. His widow Lucinda stayed on and worked the farm herself with William, who remained at the farm and eventually inherited it himself. In 1891, William and his mother managed with the help of a domestic servant and a farm servant. By 1901, William was running the farm himself with his wife Amelia and small children, William aged nine and three-year-old Elda. The census for 1911 cites the number of rooms in the farmhouse: nine, not counting bathrooms, sculleries, offices, lobbies and landings. William was 49, Amelia was 48. Their son William, aged 19, helped with the farm. Their daughter Elda was a 13-year-old schoolgirl. There was a 40-year-old farm servant George Andrews to help on the farm, predominantly a dairy farm.

William Withey died in 1923 leaving his widow Amelia £4,261/3/10d. His son, also named William Withey, in turn worked Cole House. By the time he died in 1963 the name of the property had been changed to Lake Farm. He left £15,598/15/3d and the farm eventually passed to a relative of his mother, a Mr R W Young of Stanton Drew. In 2002, Mr Young sold the farm with permission to restore and alter it to form two dwellings.

Even by 2002 no services had been connected and the house had been empty for some while. However, restoration and redevelopment were undertaken and, in 2005, the old farmhouse, divided into three units, was put up for sale. A survey made by the late Commander E H D Williams of the Somerset Vernacular Buildings Research Group discovered that, although the house had earlier origins, there had been much rebuilding in the 17th century. Many of the remaining features of any age date from that period. Before the house was re-rendered prior to its sale in 2005, old stonework from some previous structure could be traced in its walls, 'quarried' from the older buildings which had once stood on the site.

A very unusual feature still in use in the end of the house called the Barn is described by him:

Against the back wall a straight flight solid baulk stairs, originally rising from the upper end of the hall, i.e. to a solar over the inner room from an open hall. Evidence for such an arrangement has frequently been seen in Somerset, but this is the first example of original stairs remaining and the first example of straight flight solid baulk stairs, others are all spiral. The upper wall between hall and solar is late brick.

Plate 4: Timber baulk stairs at Lake Farm

His conclusion regarding the medieval house was that it would have been a longhouse – cattle byre and house combined. The fact that the house had a private room upstairs, a solar as it was called, is another sign of high status.

As far as I can tell, the name of Cole House was changed to Lake Farm after World War Two. Having spent a lot of time unravelling Cole House Farm in Clevedon from Cole House in Kenn, which was also later called Cole House Farm, I can only wish it had been changed sooner. I have been fortunate in that the estate agents selling the house in its unrestored state made sure that they invited both the Clevedon Civic Society Local History Group and Clevedon and District Archaeological Society along to see the property. Both my uncle, Derek Lilly, and friend Stephen Price have shared their photographs with me. Many thanks to Jan Pearce and her family, who welcomed me into their part of the house following restoration.

Chapter 3

A touch of the Nelsons

In 1864, a wedding ceremony took place at St Andrew's Church in Clevedon. On the 15th of November, Major Ward married his cousin, Catherine Nelson Parker Toriana Blanckley. The ceremony was performed by the Reverend H Nelson Ward. Mr Phares Barrett of Clevedon supplied the wedding carriages, and the party with their family members arrived at the church in six carriages drawn by grey horses. It must have been quite a spectacle.

The bride was dressed in a white silk dress ornamented with tulle and silk cord. Annie and Horatia Mason acted as bridesmaids along with Miss Eleanor Philippa Ward (the groom's sister) and another cousin, Miss Broughton. They wore mauve dresses with white bournouse [sic] cloaks and white bonnets made of tulle. The 'bournouse' cloaks would have been modelled on the burnoose worn in North Africa, a long, full, hooded cloak. The English version was often heavily embroidered.

As you would expect from the recurring names of Horatio, Horatia and Nelson, the new husband and wife were both closely related to Admiral Lord Nelson, one of the most lasting icons of a British hero in our long history. But how did they come to marry in Clevedon?

Before the wedding, in the early 1860s, the widowed Mrs Horatia Nelson Mason had moved to Clevedon with her step daughter and two of her own daughters from East Budleigh in Devon, where she had spent the last years of her married life. By that time, there was a well-established branch line from Clevedon to the main railway line at Yatton.

The Mason family first of all moved to a house which formerly stood on the site of the Constitutional Club at the Triangle end of Kenn Road, almost opposite the railway station. It was Brookvale House, a Regency villa. Mrs Mason was one of the daughters of the Admiral's favourite sister, Kitty Matcham, so naturally her niece Catherine Blanckley, known in the family as Toriana, came to visit.

Admiral Nelson's illegitimate daughter Horatia married the Reverend Philip Ward, and their favourite son, Major William George Ward, came to Clevedon to visit Mrs Mason at the same time. He was on leave for the first time, having joined the Indian Army. He was stationed at Madras in the Staff Corps and had come from visiting his widowed mother to stay with his oldest brother, the Reverend Horatio Nelson Ward, the Vicar of Radstock, in Somerset.

Major Ward visited Mrs Mason while his cousin Toriana was staying and they fell instantly and deeply in love (as Winifred Gerin relates in her biography of his mother). They decided to marry as soon as possible and on the 4th of November applied for a special marriage licence.

Plate 5: Toriana Blanckley and William Ward, as drawn by Lily Styles

Major Ward remained at the Royal Hotel in Hill Road. (This was on the site of the Friary.) Toriana, whose mother died when she was aged three, had been adopted by her aunt Susan Moore who stayed with her at Oxford Villa in Elton Road until after the wedding. Oxford Villa is number six, Elton Road, now called Woodbury. At that time, the house would have been relatively new, Elton Road having been laid out from 1851 as a new carriage road to connect the area known as New Clevedon with the old Village at The Triangle. Until then, Highdale Road and Chapel Hill had been the sole access routes, both woefully steep for horses to manage.

On the 15th of November, 1864, the Reverend H Nelson Ward performed the ceremony for his brother and their cousin. The bride was given away by her brother, Captain Horatio Charles Nelson Blanckley of the Royal Marines. There were, reports the Weston-super-Mare Gazette and General Advertiser,19th November, '...also present many relations and friends, and the concourse of spectators was very large.'

Interest in the family of Lord Nelson was evidently still great even almost sixty years after his death. He had been honoured in his own family to the extent that almost every generation had a person named after him. My suspicion is that, had someone called out either 'Horatio' or 'Nelson' at the wedding breakfast, almost everyone would have looked up!

At the suggestion of Alan Blackmore, I looked at the marriage entry in the Register at St Andrew's Church. William Ward's mother, Horatia Ward, Lord Nelson's daughter, had signed the Register as witness, along with Susan Moore. Keith Jemison, a qualified graphologist, kindly compared her signature with another of hers which I found online and was 80% certain that it was indeed hers.

At Oxford House, where the party gathered after the wedding, Mr John Maynard, confectioner of Hill Road, provided a 'magnificent wedding breakfast' for the guests on their return from the ceremony. (Mr Maynard had built up an extensive catering business from his early beginnings in Old Church Road, where he was an innkeeper at the Crown Inn in the 1830s. He married into the Hollyman family who owned the premises, formerly a farm house. By the 1860s, he had become very well established and had built The Regent in Hill Road.)

The couple travelled on to London in the afternoon to begin their wedding tour. They returned to India where, during the next seven years, Toriana gave birth to five little girls. In 1873, she had a sixth daughter at Pinner after she and William had returned to this country for good. William's mother had moved to Pinner in 1859 after she was widowed and was no doubt very happy to have them nearby. Sadly, William died in 1878 aged only forty-eight, but Toriana lived the longest of any of her generation, dying in May 1927 at the age of ninety-two. It is likely that William's health suffered because of the harsh Indian climate.

Plate 6: The Reverend Horatio Nelson Ward

In 1865, a year after the wedding, Mrs Mason and her daughters moved to Belvedere at number one, Park Road, a house which would certainly have been quieter than the house in Kenn Road. Sadly, shortly after the move, Mrs Mason and her daughter Augusta Susan died in January 1870. They were buried in St Andrew's Churchyard.

In 1871, the census shows that the rest of Mrs Mason's family moved to Albert Villa a few doors away in Park Road, now called Wayside Cottage. The head of the little family was now Mary Eliza Mason, aged forty-six (Mrs Mason's step daughter). The youngest remaining sister was there too, Horatia, aged thirty-six, along with their servant Louisa Hemmens aged twenty. Thirty-eight-year-old Annie Mason was staying in Exeter as a visitor with a family called Northway. All of the Mason sisters were living on their own means. They rented the house for nine years and bought it at auction for £410 in 1880.

Mary Eliza Mason died in Clevedon in 1902, followed by Annie Louisa in 1916 and finally Horatia in 1927. Horatia lived to the age of ninety-three and was sincerely mourned by her friends. Her charitable works in the town were many. (At the time of her death, 4th April, 1927, she was said to be the last living great niece of Lord Nelson, but in fact Toriana Ward died on the 23rd May in the same year, aged ninety-two.)

For many years, a print of the Battle of Trafalgar which formerly belonged to the Mason family was kept in the house. It was under covenant to be sold with the building. I gather that this tradition was broken by a recent seller who tried to sell the print to the purchasers of the house. At the time they were unable to buy it.

Isn't it a great pity that the house is now divided from an important part of its history?

Plate 7: Horatia Ward

Plate 8: Toriana Blanckley in old age

Chapter 4

Song and dance and Clevedon

A surprising number of threads from stories of the collection and preservation of folk song and dance are drawn together in Clevedon at the end of the 19th century. Cecil Sharp, an early member of the Folk Song Society, married here in All Saints Church. His great friend and collaborator, the Reverend Charles Marson, son of the late Vicar of Clevedon, performed the ceremony. The Hammond brothers, noted song collectors, grew up in Clevedon and began their collecting from here. Lady Bellairs (who wrote several books under her maiden name, Blanche St John) helped to instigate several displays of traditional and courtly dance from the Esperance dancers among others, having been a dancer in her younger days.

The English Folk Dance and Song Society holds manuscripts of the songs collected by Sharp and by the Hammond Brothers at Cecil Sharp House in London, in the Vaughan Williams Memorial Library, as well as many, many others. The Library can be contacted online. They also hold the collections and publications of Cecil Sharp himself. His books are out of print but can be obtained through libraries.

Only a few songs were collected from Clevedon by Sharp: one from Miss Doveton-Brown of Park Road, who sang Lord Rendal for him, and five songs including three sea shanties donated by a local fruiterer, Thomas Hole. No connection of Mr Hole's with the sea was traceable until I found an account of his experiences on board a Bristol ship called *Avonmore*, wrecked off the coast of Chile in 1877 during an earthquake. In 1932, he spoke at length about the event to an audience composed of members of the Bristol Shiplovers' Society and fortunately an account was published in the Clevedon Mercury of January, 1932.

He described being at the wheel during the storm and how it had to be tied to keep it steady. In total, twenty-three out of twenty-four ships in that area were damaged or wrecked. The captain's wife and their three children were on board and one of the children was drowned, tied to a stewardess who also perished. When Mr Hole surfaced after the sinking, it seemed as though the whole sea was on fire. On shore there was no wind at all, or on the sea. He certainly held his audience spellbound.

At the wedding of Miss Doveton-Brown's sister Bertha, it is worth noting that Lady Bellairs, the Hammond sisters and Mr and Mrs Cecil Sharp were listed among those giving wedding presents: there would seem to have been a social circle common to them all.

The Hammond brothers were the most closely entwined with Clevedon, so we'll start with them.

The Hammond Brothers

The Hammond family came to Clevedon from Priston near Bath in 1869 when Henry Walmsley Hammond, a retired Bengal Civil Servant in poor health, needed to convalesce. He and his wife Katharine lived for a couple of years at Rutland Lodge in Linden Road with their five children, Mary, Anthony, Henry, Robert and William. William was born in Clevedon and baptised at All Saints' in January, 1871.

Sadly, Mr Hammond's health deteriorated sharply and the family quickly travelled to Madeira in 1873 to see if the milder climate would revive him. Their sixth child Isabel was baptised at All Saints' in Clevedon in January of that year. Sadly, Mr Hammond died eight days after their arrival in Madeira. Katharine Hammond came back to Clevedon where she lived in Hill Road in Scarthingwell House, which is tucked away behind the shops at numbers 12 and 12a. The supporting columns of the font at All Saints' and the flooring which surrounded it before it was moved to the Baptistery, were given by Mrs Hammond in her husband's memory

Mrs Hammond had an independent income and either bought a house or had it built for the family in Highdale Road. She named the house Pryston, after their old home near Bath. They were certainly living there in 1876, listed in the Rate Book, and were still there in 1901. The Wilderness, the home of Cecil Sharp's future wife Constance Birch, was not far away on the opposite side of the road.

Two of the Hammond boys, Henry and Robert, became interested in collecting and recording folk songs. Henry studied at Lancing College and took his degree at Corpus Christi College, Oxford. He joined the staff of Edinburgh Academy where he taught classics and became well-known for his work on educational theory. It was at the Academy that he met George Gardiner with whom he began to collect folk songs.

Henry was an excellent sportsman, excelling at football and being capped for England. Indeed, the early records of the Clevedon Association Football Club show that he and his brother Anthony were club members during the late 1880s. Anthony was on the committee in that season, joined by Robert in 1887. Robert played for the club in 1888 and 1891 and stood in as chairman in 1889.

In 1899, Henry became Director-General of Education in Rhodesia, now Zimbabwe, but during his year there his health deteriorated. He returned to England in 1900, where the restful life forced on him must have been cruelly frustrating for so active a young man, only in his early thirties.

In 1904, George Gardiner re-enters the story, when he and Henry began to collect folk songs together. In the spring of 1905, Henry and Robert Hammond made a brief visit to Minehead and travelled thence by train to the Combe Florey area, where they collected 83 songs from twelve singers, before Sharp made his visit. By June, they were writing to Lucy Broadwood of the Folk Song Society in London. She was the niece of John Broadwood, the earliest collector of folk songs in England, and already a noted collector herself and founder member of the Folk Song Society in 1898. It was she who directed the Hammond brothers to Dorset, where they travelled about by bicycle collecting 193 songs during August, September and October.

In December 1905, their mother died at All Saints' Vicarage in East Clevedon where she lived with Mary and Isabel, her adult daughters. By 1911, Mary and Isabel had moved to Eastbourne where they rented two rooms in a house.

Working almost without ceasing until 1907, the brothers collected over 900 songs, mainly from Dorset, but from a total of six counties. They had listened to 193 singers, the brothers writing down the words. Since neither they nor George Gardiner could write down the tunes, they sought help in capturing the melodies from Mr Jeboult, the organist of Holy Trinity and then St Mary Magdalene in Taunton. The brothers persisted with their work inspite of Henry's poor health, sending the last batch of songs to Miss Broadwood in November, 1906. Henry worked with Cecil Sharp on a volume of songs from Dorset, but submitted no further songs for the remaining three years of his life. In June, 1910, he died after contracting influenza after a golf match in Hoylake near Liverpool, followed by pneumonia. Robert was a member of the Folk Song Society into the 1920s, and died in Hampshire in 1937 aged 68.

Cecil Sharp

Cecil Sharp became interested in the preservation of Morris dance when he first encountered a side of Morris dancers on Boxing Day, 1899, while he and his wife Constance were staying with her mother in Headington in Oxfordshire. Two years later, he joined the Folk Song Society and, in 1902, produced *A Book of British Song for Home and School*. His next step was to begin collecting songs, but it was not until 1903 that he heard his first live folk song and recorded it in his notebook.

Plate 9: Morris dancing in the 1950s at Clevedon Community Centre

Sharp met the Reverend Charles Marson in 1889 while they were both working in Australia. Sharp had arrived there in 1882 and worked as a bank clerk and legal secretary, while Marson arrived seven years after Sharp, having worked in very poor areas in the East End of London as well as in a few richer parishes. He was a socialist, and was soon championing improvement in the ways Australian Aborigines were treated. When they met, Sharp was co-director of the Adelaide College of Music.

By 1893 they had both returned to Britain and were married and living in London with young families. Sharp was employed at Ludgrove, a private school, where he was, for a while, tutor to the sons of the Prince of Wales, later to be Edward VII. (The Royal family has remained loyal to this school, both Prince William and Prince Harry having attended it in their youth.) Marson was working hard in a slum parish in North London.

Charles Marson was named after his father who was the Vicar of Clevedon until his death in 1895. The family had lived in Clevedon since 1871 and two of them, daughters in their twenties, were buried at their father's church, St Andrew's. Charles kept in touch with the family of his father's predecessor, William Newland Pedder and, as David Sutcliffe says in his excellent biography of Marson, *The Keys of Heaven*, 'Clevedon was Charles's spiritual home. He sent his children to be educated there and to spend holidays with Miss Sophy Pedder.' Miss Pedder would always be his confidante and a trusted friend.

While Charles was working in London, Cecil Sharp became engaged to Constance Dorothea Birch, whose family lived at a house called The Wilderness in Highdale Road. Constance Birch met Sharp when he was fifteen. He was in Weston-super-Mare, being coached for his Cambridge entrance exams. Both of them were musical – Constance sang and played the violin. Indeed, in one of several albums kept by William R Stock and housed at Clevedon Library, there are small programmes preserved which show that both Constance and her sister Alice sang at entertainments held at Rycote Lodge in Albert Road, the home of Thomas Sheldon. In January, 1891, the sisters sang duets by Rubinstein, *The Wanderer's Night Song* and *Fleeting*. Alice sang *The River of the Years* by Marzials, followed by Constance with *The Year that's Awa'*. However, the 1893 programme, also from January, lists Constance as singing a song attributed in the programme to Cecil J Sharp, *Cradle Song*. Alice sang *My Love's an Arbutus* by C Villiers Stanford. The *Cradle Song* has not yet been identified, but, if it proves to be a folk song, it records Sharp's interest in the genre as being earlier than previously has been thought to be the case.

The attachment lasted for 18 years before they married, Sharp having been to Australia for ten years in the meantime. By that time, Constance was thirty and Sharp was thirty-three.

In August, 1893, they were married in All Saints' Church, East Clevedon, with Marson performing the ceremony for his friends. Marson's address at the service clarified the duties of men and women within marriage while explaining that neither was inferior to the other, rather that their roles complemented each other. As Marson wrote in one of his letters:

> I blessed the happy pair and exhorted them, and so finished the mass and the signing. Then we drove together to the 'Wilderness' and had a neat cold breakfast in the garden on a lawn amphitheatre hewn out of the rocks. Above us waved holm oaks and arbutuses, and round were beds of bright flowers, and pines, and overhead sailing white clouds - an ideal party some twenty strong.

There was also a more formal reception at The Wilderness for a hundred of the principal residents of the neighbourhood. The gifts were reported to be numerous and costly. The couple left for London where they spent their honeymoon.

They would not have been very well off, having about £450 a year between them (about £29,000 in today's money), but theirs was a happy marriage. Constance put up with poverty and ill health with patience: her husband was not an easy man, and suffered from chronic asthma after 1899. They lived in London at first, but Constance returned to Clevedon in September, 1894, for the birth of their first daughter. They had a son and two more daughters to complete their family.

Marson's health deteriorated and, in 1895, he moved to a parish in Somerset, at Hambridge. Cecil Sharp came to stay in 1903. This was where he recorded the first folk song of the 1,500 or so he was to collect during his life, *The Seeds of Love*, sung by Marson's gardener, John England. Together with Charles Marson, he would publish three volumes of his series of Somerset folk songs. Sadly, during the proof reading of the third volume, the two men fell out with each other irrevocably, the end of a friendship of seventeen years. Sharp went on to produce two more volumes of Somerset songs as well as further works on the songs of Appalachia in the United States and elsewhere, as well as collecting Morris dances and other traditional dance forms from across England.

In 1911, Sharp founded the English Folk Dance Society to promote the traditional dances through workshops held countrywide. This body merged with the Folk Song Society in 1932 to form the English Folk Dance and Song Society, which has its headquarters and an extensive archive in London.

Lady Bellairs

Lady Bellairs was Blanche St John Moschzisker, born in Exeter in October 1847 to Franz Adolphe Moschzisker (the surname is Polish, derived from Moses) and Laura St John, who married in 1844. Her father, a teacher of German, French and Hebrew, who seems to have vanished early in her life, was declared bankrupt in 1848. By 1851, her mother was alone in Exeter with Blanche and her sister Matilda. Her mother was dependent on her relatives for support, eventually listing herself as a widow in 1871. Blanche's maternal grandfather was Edward Beauchamp St John, the Vicar of Ideford, born in Madras and related to Baron St John of Bletso. The census of 1861 records that, at the age of twelve, Blanche was at a ladies' boarding school in Dawlish.

In 1867, she married Sir William Bellairs as his second wife. In due course the couple had four children, Beauchamp, Norman, Carlyon and Roger. The Bellairs moved to Clevedon in

1886 and Lady Bellairs rapidly seems to have established herself in Clevedon society as an excellent organiser.

In 1908, having triumphed with an Arts, Crafts and Industries Exhibition in Clevedon, Lady Bellairs turned her attention to dance. Together with instructors from the Esperance Club of London, and some helpers from Bristol, she initiated the training of dancers in the various surviving Morris dances. The Esperance Club was formed in the mid-1890s in London in an attempt to give girls working in unpleasant conditions in the dressmaking industry some pleasant exercise. In September, 1905, one of the founders, Mary Neal, became very interested in the work of Cecil Sharp and taught the girls the steps of the Morris dances. The troupes formed by women at this time did much to promote the dances and their preservation.

The Clevedon Morris side was among the earliest revival sides, although they are no longer in existence. Some dances, both Morris and country, were performed at a fair in the 1950s at Clevedon Community Centre and photographed by Ted Caple and another local man (see Plate 10). The Morris side was re-formed for a while in 1983 by some of the Clevedon Coastguards.

The earlier beginnings of Clevedon Morris would seem to lie in Lady Bellairs' determination to show Clevedon just how much folk dance and song was being brought back to life in Britain. On the 22nd of February 1908, there was a performance in the Public Hall at Sixways by a troupe largely formed of sons and daughters of tradesmen of Upper Clevedon.

Among them were Gretchen Wickenden, daughter of Alfred B. Wickenden of the bakery at Regent House. After becoming a professional singer, she married William A. Nichols, who was also involved with this group, as were his brother Frederick and sisters Florence and Dorothy. The Nichols were the children of Susan Nichols who, after her husband Frederick died, moved out of the Post Office at 12 Hill Road and started a stationery business at number 81. Her daughters continued the business into the late 1940s.

Ethel Lovegrove was related to family who ran a shop in Marine Parade next door to the Higgs family who owned a drapery shop there. She married A. V. Higgs, a pianist, also with this group. His brother Stuart Higgs continued to run the drapery shop.

The Sweet family were bakers at Reading House in Alexandra Road and their relative, Nellie, was performing in 1908. Also involved was J. H. Winsor, who worked with them in their bakery.

Gertrude Luff lived with her parents in Wellington Terrace where they kept a boarding house. Her brother William was performing too. Chrissie Dyer worked at the family dairy at Kenn Court Farm. The family sold their milks, eggs and cheese at Kenn Court Dairy in Alexandra Road. Ruth Counsell lived in Yatton and was an assistant photographer, possibly working in Clevedon with Edwin Hazell in Linden Road.

Tryphena Parker was the daughter of John Bartholomew Parker, another Hill Road businessman, with a large grocery shop at Handel House. Gerald Tyers was a bank clerk living in Bellevue Road and Edward D'Arcy Burbidge was in partnership with Mr Trestrail in a solicitors' office in Hill Road.

It was Major Trestrail who arranged the loan of a costume for the hobby horse from the Prince's Theatre in Bristol. Messrs Stephens of Hill Road made the costume for the jester as well as adding a little more to the hobby horse's brightly coloured garb. The Major also acted as stage manager.

The teacher employed for the occasion was Rose Mallett, one of the finest that the Esperance Club could offer. She was so successful that the event was put on sooner than had been planned, in February. Miss Mallett danced the Bacca Pipes jig which was very well received.

In May, the performer put on a second show adding dances such as *Old Mother Oxford*, *The Old Woman Tossed Up in a*

Blanket and *Rodney* to the programme. Miss Mallett again assisted with rehearsals, but did not dance herself on this occasion.

The group called themselves the Somerset Morris Dancers, performing on Tuesday and Thursday afternoons and evenings. On the Wednesday, the afternoon was devoted to the Misses Parnall, with their Nation and Fancy Costume dances, while in the evening there was a concert of old sea shanties. No doubt the songs collected for Sharp from Tommy Hole were included.

Lady Bellairs announced at the second concert that she would be organising a fund-raising event for the Crimea veterans, her husband having served throughout the entire campaign without one day of leave This event went ahead in July, 1908, with the Somerset Morris Dancers performing again. By that time, Miss Wickenden had moved away and was a singer, staying with her sister in Lewisham. The rest of the group was largely the same as before.

The next event to feature traditional and historic dance was a fête which took place at Clevedon Court in 1912, with Lady Bellairs featuring largely on the organising committee. Her daughter-in-law, Veronica Beatrice Bellairs, arranged dancing entertainments at that fête along with the Misses Parnall of Clifton, including the Pavane, a formal, stately dance performed at court and elsewhere during the 16th and 17th centuries. The Misses Parnall were the daughters of William and Eliza Parnall, who owned a weighing machine factory in Bristol, part of Parnall and Sons, a very extensive shop-fitting company. Two of their daughters, Edith and Muriel, were involved with teaching various forms of dance. By 1907, Edith had married, but Muriel was still teaching dance in 1911 from Clifton where she lived with her widowed mother.

Fifteen dancers were in the group arranged by the Parnalls and the dance proved to be quite a spectacle. A large marquee had been hired for the performance and the Pavane was danced there by eight of the ladies. Also on the programme was a varied offering of popular pieces.

Plate 10: Country dance in the 1950s at Clevedon Community Centre

The pupils of Miss Dunford's School took part and mastered country dances such as *Jenny Pluck Pears* and *Pop Goes the Weazel* among many others. Then Jack Winsor and Reginald House led them in playing traditional children's games as well as maypole dances. Miss Agnes Mary Dunford was the daughter of the landlady of the Old Inn. She founded Wycliffe School in Seavale Road which eventually moved to Linden Road where it continued as a successful small private school for girls until the second half of the 20th century. As in 1908, many of the children dancing came from families who ran shops in Clevedon – small private schools were within the price bracket they could afford.

It seems that, by 1912, the absence of the influence of Miss Gretchen Wickenden had reduced the number of Morris dancers and that several other dancers of the 1908 season had moved away from Clevedon. The town's association with the folk dance and song revival, for the time being, was coming to an end.

Chapter 5

Dowlais Farm

Dowlais Farm lies on Lower Strode Road, off Southern Way, and even today is quite remote from the town. In 1919, when the Clevedon Court Estate sold off a large number of farms and cottages, Dowlais was purchased by the local authority and the land was split into smallholdings with new houses to be rented to men returning from the Great War. The house remained as it was, but with less land to its name.

For many years the origin of the name of the farm was unknown. There is a Welsh settlement of that name near Merthyr Tydfil and it is also the name of a coarse linen cloth from Doulas in Brittany. How could either of those names have become attached to a farm in Somerset? The answer emerged in one of the deeds and leases found stuffed in a chimney in half a dozen sacks at Clevedon Court in the early 1960s. It was the name of a tenant, Mr Dowless.

Mr Dowless held the farm in 1700 when Walter Greene of Walton Park purchased much of the Clevedon Manor before selling it on to the Elton family of Clevedon Court. Previous to his ownership, though, who had the farm? A search among documents I have transcribed over the years has brought some of the answers to this question to light.

Because many of the leases described where the area listing known fields to the north, south, east and west, I have been able to identify fields held by several tenants of the farm house and lands. Records I have used are the Tithe Map, Census Returns, town directories, Rate lists, Land Tax and more. Many of these have been transcribed by my uncle, Derek Lilly, who has shared his work with many besides me. I also use the Ancestry website, which is a very helpful resource.

Beginnings

The Tithe Map, made in 1839 when Tithe payments were commuted, shows Dowlais Farm where it is today. However, there is a small plot adjoining the house to the west where previously there stood another house.

These two houses were known in the 17th century as Easthouse and Westhouse – despite their not very exciting names, the houses have interesting histories.

A Survey, completed in 1630 and undertaken for Elizabeth Wake when she decided to sell Clevedon Manor after her husband's death, lists all the houses belonging to the Manor, giving the ages of the people whose lives they were held for, their names, the condition of the houses, rents, incomes and so forth. This is where the known history of Dowlais Farm begins.

At that time, the two houses were held by John Perry and Dorothy Perry, each house being described as 'good' in the Survey. John held his lease with two other 'lives', Edward and Joan. This was an ancient form of lease in which the named persons, or 'lives', held the lease as long as one of them was still living, or for 99 years. Any buildings erected on the property by the time the lease finished would then revert to the original owner, along with the land.

Dorothy Perry was the only person named in her lease. She held 66 acres of land as well as half a warth, land alongside the sea measuring 50 acres, which we now call the Saltings. John held 60 acres of land and the other half of the warth, also 50 acres. Each of the farms brought in over £4 a year. Both, if one of the lives named died, had to give the Lord of the Manor one of the best beasts on the farm to cover the expense of reissuing the lease. Later documents clarify that Dorothy had the house to the west and John the house to the east.

Because the church registers have not survived in these

early years for Clevedon, it can be difficult to work out how the Perrys were related to each other. Luckily, in 1653, the house to the east was re-leased and we can find out more about the family living in Dowlais Farm. They held Easthouse with two bartons (barnyards) adjoining it, with 56 acres of land consisting of fields called Cowlease, Riddie Mead, Oxenlease, Twelve Acres, and One Acre as well as a half share, or moiety, in land alongside the sea called Wickham's Wharf.

This gives a lot of extra information, including the fact that the house had two barnyards, or bartons. The name Easthouse shows that we are definitely on the right track in thinking that this is Dowlais Farm, shown on the Tithe Map with an empty plot where the neighbouring house once stood. Most of the field names can be identified on the Tithe Map too. The land totals 56 acres, so it is likely that we are looking at the house held in 1630 by John Perry. I take it that he died, leaving his son Edward to continue the lease. Edward had adult children, John, Joan and Edward Perry the younger. In this document, Joan and Edward the younger were already named as lives, and their father was altering the lease I believe, to add his son John's name in his place.

Only the following year, in 1654, there was turmoil for the Perrys when the Earl of Bristol, the Lord of the Manor, terminated their lease owing to the great expense he had borne having work carried out to maintain the sea wall on their western boundary, which they had allowed to fall into disrepair.

The Perrys had to give up the house and barnyards or hand back Cowlease or, a third alternative, to pay £150 for one portion, £30 for the other and an annual rent of £2.6d.

The Earl had quit claimed – which means that John Perry would otherwise lose the lease altogether. Terrible problems with the sea wall and its maintenance are a continuing theme, as we will see.

In 1656, a further investigation into the income of the Manor was made resulting in a document called a Rental that showed that John Perry still held half of Wickham's Warth at a rent of £8/5/0d a year. The other half was held by John Knight, later Sir John, who eventually held several more large properties in Clevedon and was Mayor of Bristol. He took a seven-year lease from 1656. West House became known as Knight's Tenement in the Marsh.

In 1881, Mr Green, an archaeologist, visited Clevedon along with members of Somerset Archaeological and Natural History Society. They visited Clevedon Court and also walked around parts of the town. Here is an extract from the written account published in the Society's Proceedings for 1881:

Passing through the meadow by the sea, Mr Green gave an episode of some litigation about the repairs of the sea wall. It seemed that there was in Clevedon a farm, known as Perry's Marsh Farm, worth about £80 a year, and there belonged to it a large piece of ground called The Warth adjoining the sea shore by the Severn, but about seven feet higher than the shore, forming a natural bank of earth against the sea, and which had never been repaired by anybody.

Within this marsh ground was a ditch and a bank cast up about three feet high, forming a second barrier. The sea breaking in, in 1667, destroyed the outer bank, and carried away about four score acres several feet in depth, and not only were the other forty acres left threatened with a like destruction, but the marsh land further in was also in danger. The question was who should repair it. As the owners of the shore land refused to do so, an action was brought in the Exchequer by the inland owners, who alleged that it was from carelessness on the part of the shore owners from not keeping out the 'woose' soil brought down by the river that the wall then lay 'lacerated and worn down.

The owners disagreed and claimed that all the landowners should pay towards the sea wall repairs, because the wall protected all of the land. The court decreed that this was right, but the plaintiffs, not liking the judgement, refused obedience and, as local magnates, endeavoured to intimidate their opponents by inflicting a heavy fine for their asserted neglect. The consequence was that Mr William Strode and others of the more inland owners found themselves committed to 'ye p'son of ye flete' (Fleet Prison) for their contempt.

On their bringing another action (Michaelmas, 33rd Chas II, ie 1681–2), the former decree was confirmed. At the end of a long account occupying thirteen skins of parchment written on both sides, Mr Strode and the others were ordered to be freed, and their bonds for £400 to be cancelled. *(Exchequer Decrees Mich 27th Chas II, 1675–1676, page 208. Exchequer Decrees, page 311)*

So, even in 1667, thirteen years after the Perrys had to release the farm because of their neglect of the sea wall, there was still a great problem from inundation by the sea. The case took until 1673 to be resolved. Three years after that, in 1676, the whole sea wall question was addressed by the Manor. This record, too, is held by Somerset Record Office, reference number dd/en/104.

The sea wall was known as the 'west sea wall'; the moor wall, now partly the lane known as Nailsea Wall, was called the 'east sea wall'. Mr Perry had five feet of the east sea wall to maintain, and sixteen feet of the sea wall itself, the west sea wall. It must have been a great relief to him not to have the entire stretch of sea all along his boundaries to repair.

The Earl of Bristol had lost Clevedon after the Civil War when it was confiscated and given to the son of Sir Walter Raleigh. However, he regained it after the Restoration of Charles II and had much work to do repairing – yet again – the sea wall. This time he made what we would call a proper job of it. From February, 1682 to September, 1683, Bristol Channel sailing vessels, known as 'trows', brought stone to the sea banks. Drink was bought for the 'sailers', and local men were paid to build the wall and dig out some silted up areas of Clevedon Pill. Poles were set up as sea marks – I assume these were to give an idea of what height the wall needed to be. The entire bill came to £427/14/5d. Given that a 99-year lease for a cottage only cost £2/10s, this was a very large sum of money. After this, a new agreement was made with all the leaseholders to clarify that everyone paid for a certain length of each of the walls.

The farm is next referred to in a purchase of Clevedon Manorial lands made by Walter Greene of Walton Park. He bought a vast acreage of land and farmhouses in 1700, including the house and garden, twelve acres in several pieces and a meadow called Twelve Acres, all called 'Dowless his tenement'. The seawalls had to be repaired from Phelps rails to Hicks Warth, and a sluice called the Gout, or Ear, had to be kept in good repair too. *(1700 Somerset Record Office, dd/en/5)*

This is the time when the farm was given its present-day name – the phrase, 'Dowless his tenement', tells us that the tenant was a Mr Dowless who had taken the farmholding before this document of 1700 and after John Perry vacated it – at some unknown point in the late 17th century. The same document lists the house next door, West House, also called Knight's Marsh House, as being roofless, so this was the point when that house had begun to sink slowly away. When quarrying and carting stone cost money, fallen houses came in as a useful resource for stone for outbuildings or repairs, which is how houses come to disappear.

In 1709, Walter Green sold his lands to the Elton family, and, in that lease, it seems that John Perry kept back some land for himself, while Mr Dowless continued to lease Dowlais with several fields. *(ibid.)*

By that time, both Dowless and Knight's had been rented to a man called John Player for three years. Sir Abraham Elton recorded in a lease of 1712 that Mr Edward Sesse was renting both properties for a further four years, 'on the same termes and conditions', except that he had to pay Mr Player a small amount of interest for his work on the buildings so far. Mr Sesse paid a rent of £112.

Mr Sesse, or Sess, was taking over the house Mr Player had built at 5% interest while the outbuildings mentioned were free of charge. Presumably the original house had suffered the ravages of time and needed extensive work. He only enjoyed the house for ten years, as he died in 1722 in Kingston Seymour leaving a sum of money to establish a charity in his name:

> Sess Charity. Real estate of the late Edward Sess, heretofore of parish of Kingstone Seymour; - charged with payment of twenty shillings: object, to pay on the twelfth day of (no month given) every year the sum of 10s for the preaching of a sermon, and the other 10s to be given to the second poor of the said parish.' *[Accounts and papers, 7 volumes, volume 3, relating to charities and charitable donations for the benefit of the poor and other persons in England and Wales. Session 5, Feb -24, June 1829.]*

Richard and Samuel Eyres took the lease from the Eltons after Mr Sesse died. The brief transcript I have made lists all of the land they leased with it:

> 1722
> 3 farms, Knights, Dowlesses and Beakes, all in Clevedon, for one year
> Rent £147/10/-
> 2 messuages or tenements called Knights and Dowlesses Warth Tenements, together with,4 acres meadow or pasture in Dugnam adjoining 40 Acres Lane, 23 acres called Wickfield, the Inner Warth, formerly Canhams containing 15 acres, ground

called the Outer Warth, land called Dowless containing 20 acres, 3 acres adjoining Dowless tenement, Readymead containing 15 acres, The Leaze containing 14 acres, 3 acres of Dowless tenement formerly Roger Stone, afterwards John Player and John Russell and late and now Edward Sesse

All belonging to Dowless

Also;

5 acres meadow formerly belonging to Clevedon Mill and now or late of John Player, and a close of meadow or pasture called 40 Acres, late Wm Horwood, late Edward Sesse and now Elizabeth Stone

Also Beakes Tenement late Elizabeth Stone.'
(1722 Somerset Record Office, dd/en/95)

Some of the land names in the 1722 lease might explain the inner and outer bounds later referred to in the 1738 lease – perhaps they were the Inner Warth and Outer Warth indirectly referred to in the Exchequer case, the two sea banks edging the property. Clevedon Mill, incidentally, was sited on the sea wall and driven by the tide. By this time it was beginning to fall into disrepair.

It seems that the next person to lease Dowlais, along with lands called Tysons, was John Hollyman. He was a member of a family which had moved to Clevedon in the late 17th century and bought several farms in the Manor. John Hollyman died in 1736 and the holding had passed back to the Elton family. During his time at the farm he served as Church warden, as did many other members of his family at various times. No other trace of his tenancy survives, but he is named as the previous landholder when the house and land passed in 1738 to William Wilmot.

Mr Wilmot's lease of 1738 has suffered from its time spent up a chimney in a sack, but it is possible to see that fields called

Tysons, Wickfield and Smiths were included in his holdings. Also that taxes payable by him were the Window Tax and Poor Tax. He was to maintain the 'in bounds' and pay the tythes at 4d an acre to the parish church, St Andrew's. The Eltons would pay the Land Tax and the Church Rates and keep the 'out bounds'. *(Somerset Record Office dd/en/108)*

As happens with records, there is a gap now until Dowlais turns up again in the Land Tax where it is recorded that Sir Abraham Elton, followed by his brother, Sir Abraham Isaac Elton, paid the Tax in the late 1760s until a second William Wilmot, perhaps a relative of the earlier man, took over and farmed at Dowlais from 1770 until 1779. William Coombs took over from him and farmed there on his own until 1791 when part of the land was shared with Daniel Hayman. Mr Hayman seems to have ducked out of this arrangement after a few years and William Gregory took over Hayman's former share of Dowlais in 1797. Thomas Coombs succeeded William Coombs in 1803 and continued to share land with, oddly enough, Thomas Gregory instead of William Gregory!

Five years later, in 1808, John Griffin is tenant for the Coombs' former part of Dowlais, still sharing with Thomas Gregory. In 1811, at last a familiar person appears, William Hollyman, the Steward of the Clevedon Court Estate who took over from John Griffin. The Hollyman family, as I said earlier, had moved to Clevedon as farmers in the late 17th century. They rapidly expanded their land holdings farming in Kenn Road, Old Church Road, Old Street and indeed at Clevedon's chief farm, Highdale Farm, which lay north of Old Street. Today the best landmark for this farmhouse is Christ Church, the house being tucked into the hillside below the church.

William was the youngest son of Thomas Hollyman, the only child born to Thomas and his second wife, Hannah Wall. William had no fewer than ten older half-siblings from his father's first marriage. He played a great part as administrator of the

Clevedon Court Estate as Clevedon was being developed by the Elton family as a select seaside resort after 1820. He built the very first Regency-style houses in the growing town, at East Clevedon Triangle in 1821, Ilex House and Trellis House, followed by many more. His half-brother Thomas was landlord of the Old Inn and extended his business in the early 1820s to the Rock House, now below the Royal Pier Hotel on The Beach.

William Hollyman died in 1850 aged only fifty-nine, having made a remarkable impact on the town. He farmed a share of the land at Dowlais but did not live there. Thomas Gregory only continued until 1813 at which point William farmed the entire holding for the following years, sharing with his brother John from 1817 until 1824, when his involvement ceased and he concentrated on speculative building, notably erecting the Royal Hotel in Hill Road in 1825, where the Friary now stands.

John Hollyman stayed on at Dowlais, though in 1827 he was sharing with Nicholas Cottle. By 1832, Mr Cottle had secured the whole of Dowlais and its lands and the Cottle family stayed there until the late 19th century.

At this point, because Census Returns were introduced recording who had slept at the house the night previous to the collector of information calling with his forms, it is possible to find out far more about who actually lived at Dowlais. The 1841 Census only records a few details, but in every tenth year more information was gradually taken as the census taker made his rounds. The first Census of 1831 only recorded numbers of people and even nationally very little survives from that year. From 1841, though, the records are preserved and we are able to gain a greater insight into the lives of the family and their servants living at the farm.

In 1841 at Dowlais, Nicholas Cottle and his wife Elizabeth, both in their thirties, lived with their children, Ann aged twenty, Elizabeth aged fifteen, William aged five and Emily aged four. Ellen Harber lived with them, aged nine, and they had a servant aged fifteen, Charlotte Wilkins.

Ten years later, the 1851 Census added exact ages (instead of to the nearest five years), as well as places of birth. Nicholas was born at Chelvey near Nailsea in 1801 and farmed 150 acres. Another daughter, Harriet aged twenty-one, was at home with her family, though I haven't been able to trace her whereabouts in 1841. Ann had left home and was working as a governess for the Honourable Margaret Nugent Jones at Hinton Charterhouse on the Mendips. Elizabeth was a drapery assistant in Bristol, lodging near St Mary le Port. Still living at home with their parents and Harriet were Emily aged thirteen and William aged eighteen. There were two servants, Hannah Carfield aged thirteen and Samuel Collins aged eighteen.

Members of the family still living at home with Nicholas and Elizabeth in 1861 were William aged twenty-eight and Emily aged twenty-three, Harriet having married in 1854. There was one servant in this year sleeping at the house, Grace Young aged seventeen, listed as a farm servant, which may mean she helped with some of the farm work such as milking and helping with dairy work. Nicholas still farmed 150 acres and employed three men on the farm.

Nicholas retired before 1871 and he and Elizabeth were living in part of Knap House in Chapel Hill. William Cottle, aged thirty-six, had taken over Dowlais Farm. He had married Anna Maria Morris from Backwell, a former dairymaid. Her brother, William Morris, worked with William as farm assistant and their farm servant was Charles Neads. The size of the farm is not mentioned at all, but I would assume it to be the same as before, one of the larger farms of the Manor.

Nicholas died in 1874, followed by Elizabeth five years later. They left under £3,000, but this was a fairly substantial amount of money for William to inherit. By 1881, William was forty-nine, ten years older than his wife Anna. By that time, they had five children, Reginald aged eight, Ernest aged seven, Beatrice aged five, Francis aged four and Henry aged two, the four older children all being at school. William Morris was still working on the farm along with a general servant, Mary Ann Payne.

In 1891, the situation was much the same, with all the children still at home. The three oldest were no longer at school, the two boys being occupied as farmer's sons – probably helping around the farm and learning their trade. Beatrice had no occupation listed but, I am sure, would have been given something to do to help her mother. Francis and Henry were still at school, joined by eight-year-old Gerald. It is interesting to see a wider range of forenames emerging from the 1870s onwards superseding the traditional John, William, Sarah, Mary and so on! There are no resident servants in this census.

When William Cottle died, Anna moved to Milton, part of Weston-super-Mare near Kewstoke, where she and her children continued to farm. In 1895, Henry Sweet and his wife Agnes took Dowlais Farm. Tragically, during a flood of the area in February, 1899, Mrs Sweet insisted on driving to Seawall Farm (further south in Lower Strode Road, but in Kingston Seymour) to see if relatives there were safe. The trap overturned and she was drowned.

Dowlais Farm was occupied in 1901 by Henry Sweet and his widowed sister, Ann Lewis. (It is interesting to know that one of their sisters married Frederick Parker, who had a noted bakery in Kenn Road. Also in the confectionery line was their brother Francis Sweet, who opened a bakery in Copse Road in the 1860s, moving to the newly built Reading House in Alexandra Road in 1882 to continue his business. The bakery became a pub, the Reading House – the Sweets chose that name because, according to his nephew, they stocked Huntley and Palmer's Reading biscuits *[Clevedon Mercury, 6 February, 1976]*. After the sign was repainted to show a man reading there was some confusion about this – especially as the public library was based a few doors away from the Reading House when it was first set up!)

Returning to Henry Sweet himself, the occupations of his farm servants are listed fully in the 1901 Census Return. Thus, we can gain more of an idea of the nature of the farming at Dowlais. Harriet Parnell was the dairywoman, John Diment the farm carter, Elizabeth Perkins was a domestic servant, Richard Locke was cow man and Arthur Winsor looked after the pigs – with dairying and pigs as well, a fairly safe, broad-based programme. Henry did not stay long in Clevedon it seems: he was back in Kingston Seymour in 1911 and died in Wiltshire in 1924.

In 1910, Ernest Walter House is given as the farmer at Dowlais in Kelly's Trade Directory. His census details in 1911 show that he was forty, his wife Ada forty-two and that they had a son, Leonard, aged seventeen working on the farm with his father. The dairy assistant was Margaret Atkins from Plymouth and a farm labourer, nineteen-year-old John Richards also lived in. The Census in this year asked how many rooms there were in the house, counting the kitchen, but not counting scullery, landing, lobby, closet or bathroom. Dowlais Farm had eight rooms. Mr House, born in Biddisham in Somerset, was not related to Oliver House the shoemaker or to Frank House the dairyman, both of whom were already in Clevedon.

Ernest W. House appears in the 1923 Directory at Dowlais Farm. In the following year, he moved to Exeter House in Old Church Road where, in partnership with Mr Clements, he ran a shop that sold fish and game. If you stand in Queen's Road and look across to the left hand corner of Lower Queen's Road, even now you'll see an advertisement painted on the gable above the corner shop.

Mr House was able to remain at the farm after the Clevedon Court Estate sale of 1919, either because he bought the property or because he had the tenancy. Ten other farms, land and 64 cottages were sold as well – after the Great War, half of England changed hands, either because of death duties or the general economic slump. Clevedon was no exception.

Lot. 4. DOWLAIS FARM.

Plate 11: Dowlais Farm, 1919

1919 First Clevedon Court Estate Sale
Lot 4
The highly desirable rich grazing farm known as
Dowlais Farm, with its alluvial pasture, orchard and
arable land, saltings and a modern cottage,
containing a total area of 155 acres 2 rods and 20
perches, more particularly described as follows;
708 House, buildings and garden
707 Orchard
204 The 12 Acres
part 202 Cottage and garden
part 202 Home 6 Acres
203 Frontage
696 Home Ground
695 Part of the 3 Acres
695a Part of the 3 Acres

697 The 4 Acres
702 The 9 Acres
703 Old Garden and Drove
700 The 12 Acres
699 Ruddy Mead
690 Ox Lease
689 Cannons
691 Mill Ground
682 Cannons
701 The 30 Acres
718 Salt Wharf

The farmhouse, built of stone and slated, contains a lobby, 2 sitting rooms, kitchen, dairy, milk house and boiler house on the ground floor; on the first floor are 4 bedrooms and 2 cheese rooms; large attic. There is a good covered court.

The cottage contains 2 rooms and a washhouse on ground floor and 3 rooms over. Privy in garden.

The outbuildings include w.c. with flush cistern, cider house and implement house, cattle shed with loft over, 3-stall stable with loft over, waggon house, trap house, root house with loft over, bull house, 2 sheds for 39 cattle, 2 calves' houses, loose house, meal house, piggeries, men's closet, coal house and root house. On field no. 689 is a stone and tile lock-up shed known as the Gullhouse.

The following buildings are the property of the tenant:- greenhouse, calves' house, engine-house, implement-shed and 2 Dutch barns, with the exception of the posts of the Dutch barn east of the farmhouse, poultry-house.

Company's water is laid on to the house, buildings and yard.

By agreement dated 7th July 1902, the Clevedon Water Company undertook to provide and maintain a water supply to Dowlais farm and certain other premises belonging to the Vendor, in consideration of a total payment of £20 p.a. in addition to the customary charges for water; the proportion of the said payment of the said £20 p.a. payable by the purchaser of the lot has, by arrangement with the Company, been fixed at £6 13s 4d p.a., and the purchaser shall be required to sign an agreement with the Company to pay this amount; this agreement shall be in a form which may be inspected at Messrs. J.P. Sturge & Sons' office during office hours on the 3 days preceding the sale.

A right of way is reserved over the Old Garden and Drove for the benefit of Lot 33 (The 40 Acres).

The necessary rights of access to the Sea Wall are reserved.

A small part of this lot is subject to a Lease to the Somerset Territorial Force Association for 14 years, from 25th March 1910, of the right to make and use the Rifle Range at a total rent of £22 p.a.. The proportion of the said rent payable to the purchaser of this lot is fixed at £15 p.a. The targets, etc., on Cannons, are the property of the Somerset Territorial Force Association, subject to the provisions of the said Lease. A copy of the Lease can be seen at Messrs J.P. Sturge and Sons' office, 11 Orchard St, Bristol, during the 3 days preceding the sale.

This lot is let to Mr E W House at a rent of £315 p.a., less £15 allowed for the Rifle range; the tenant pays £9 p.a. in addition for the cottage.

Timber, £39. Commuted Tithe, £31 16s 1d.

I find the most startling thing about the list of fields is that many of them are those held by the farm in 1653, viz: Riddie Mead, 15 acres pasture; Oxenlease, 14 acres; Ground called Twelve acres; Wickhams Wharth, 60 acres.

The fields called Cannons get their name from their tenant in the 1700s, Mr Keinham or Canham, not from any later association with the Volunteer Artillery based on Wain's Hill after 1860. The artillery fired their cannon across the Pill at target barrels moored in the bay. The Rifle Range was based there, as mentioned in the 1919 sale.

Somerset County Council purchased Dowlais Farm and divided it into eight small land holdings with new farmhouses on them so that men returning from service in the Great War could be given the opportunity to take up farming. The overall plan for the project was drawn up in 1920.

Mr House moved on in 1923, as I have said, and the new man at Dowlais in 1924 was Arthur John Parker, who was still there when the last Kelly's Directory I can find was published in 1939.

By 2017, Dowlais Farm had been occupied by Neville and Angela Hughes for some thirty years. The house was sold in this year to begin a new chapter with new owners, who kindly showed me the house in chaotic conditions. Dowlais has a new lease of life with them.

Chapter 6

Hide Hall: Clevedon's oldest farm

Now known as Highdale Farm, this large farmhouse rebuilt on an ancient site in the late 17th century lies above Highdale Avenue and below Highdale Road. It can be seen from the steep pathway which descends from the kissing gate by Christchurch in Highdale Road. Its original name was Hide Hall and it sits between the Norman Church of St Andrew's on the coast and Clevedon Court on the Tickenham Road.

The earliest reference to the site dates from the Patent Rolls of 1297 when there was a chantry chapel there, run by a priest called Hugh of Wenlock. A chantry chapel could be established by a wealthy person who endowed it with an income (often from land given to be rented out) so that masses could be said for their soul. As the church here at Clevedon was certainly not in a central position, Hide Hall would have been very much frequented by parishioners who could attend the chapel for mass on all but the four major services of the Church year.

The chapel may have been an independent building, but it is probable that it was within a house or attached to it. With a name like Hide Hall it is extremely likely that there was a house here for the Manorial Steward, or Reeve, who would have managed the allocation of work on farm land in the Manor. A hide is an ancient measurement of land and the name suggests strongly that the house was used by a person responsible for managing large areas of land. In the Bishop's Registers kept by the Diocese of Bath and Wells, the names of chaplains at Hide Hall, or Hydall as it soon became known, are recorded:

1318 William de Godyneland
1349 Thomas de Sulihull

1351 Roger de Etyndon
1377 William Dorsete exchanged with Richard Tyntewell
1377 in December, William Hanley
1380 John Gryme.

I shall use Hide Hall through the rest of the text, for clarity.

Hide Hall makes its next appearance in two published collections of records of the Abbey and Convent of St Augustine in Bristol, to which Clevedon, among several other parishes in North Somerset, had been transferred during the 13th century. In both *Two Compotus Rolls of St Augustine's Abbey, Bristol for 1491-2 and 1511-12* and *'Some Manorial Accounts of St Augustine's Abbey Bristol being the computa of the Manors for 1491-2 and 1496-7 and other documents of the fifteenth and sixteenth centuries*, published by Bristol Record Society, it is recorded under the name of Edyesplace in Clevedon, paying in both sets of accounts £2 a year rent to the Abbey and Convent of St Augustine in Bristol, now Bristol Cathedral.

In 1534, Henry VIII ordered a Survey of Chantries as part of the Dissolution of various Roman Catholic foundations during the formation of the Church of England. There was at Hide Hall, after the chantries were dissolved, a priest called Robert who lived on the income from lands rented out to be farmed at £6/8/2d per annum. The usual tenth was deducted from this for the Church itself, the sum being 12s/10d.

During the reign of Henry VIII, William Parsons of Clevedon leased a field belonging to Hide Hall from Robert Iring, presumably the priest above, for the term of Robert's life. Poor Mr Parsons evidently had an appalling time at the hands of John Bulbeck who had taken the lease for the rest of the farm land. There is no precise year given for this dispute, the details of which I have rendered into modern English.

William Parsons asked that the case should be judged by the Court of Star Chamber:

Most humbly begging of your Highness your poor
and daily orator William Parsons of Clevedon in
your County of Somerset, husbandman, that whereas
one Robert Iring, clerk was seized of a certain
chantry in and within the Chapel of Hydall in
Clevedon aforesaid called the chantry of Hydall and
of certain lands and tenements pertaining to the
same chantry for him and to his successors as
chantry priests of the same chantry.

Robert Iringe being in possession, granted a
certain close of pasture called the West Nine Acres
in Clevedon for the term of his Robert Iringe's life.
William Parsons has been paying the said Robert
13s 4d a year for the pasture for 16 years or
thereabouts until one John Bulbecke of Clevedon,
gentleman, John Badham or Bodham of Clevedon,
'syngngman' and Robert Avery of Clevedon
'fonyngman' with some others they had gathered
entered the field last December on the 10th with
swords and shields and forest bills [ie billhooks].
They drove out two oxen the property of William
Parsons.

The said John Bulbecke and others with him
assaulted Alice Parsons, William Parsons' wife,
with their weapons and wounded her head, which
left her ill and danger of losing her life for more than
two months. After which William Parsons re-entered
the field and placed some of his beasts and cattle
there again.

After a month Robert Avery and John Lovell
of Clevedon, husbandman and Thomas Collins of
Clevedon, husbandman entered the field on the 17th
January last with their swords, staves and other
weapons and entered the field on John Bulbecke's

behalf. They carried away five cows great with calf belonging to William Parsons and beat them, which caused three calves to be lost.

Since then, John Bulbecke has continued to keep William Parsons out of the field contrary to good practice. And to the ruin of William Parsons, unless your highness of your abundant grace will raise a writ of subpoena against John Bulbecke, Robert Avery and John Badham commanding them to appear in the Court of Star Chamber, there to be ordered to to abide by your highness' direction.
And your orator shall pray for the preservation of your highness daily in health and prosperity long to endure.

After Henry VIII's death in 1547, his son Edward VI continued the last stages of the Dissolution and ordered a Second Survey of Chantries in 1548. The description reads:

one messuage within the towne of Clyvedon with all and singular landes, meadowes and pastures and fedinge thereunto belonging letten to farme to John Bulbecke for term of sixty three years by Indenture dated 12th day of March in the 26th yeare [1534/5] of the reigne of our late souvraigne lorde King Henry VIII. Plate and ornaments therein none. Memor: Ther hath ben neyther incumbent nor other mynister resident upon the said free chapell syns the date of the foresaide Indenture, but the lessee receyveth the proffets of the same to his owen use as may appere by the first booke of Survey of College Chantries &c and there is nothing presented concerning the free chapell at the last Survey, howsoever the matter goeth.

John Bulbeck was the grandson of William Bulbeck, who is recorded in the Visitations for the County of Somerset in 1531 and 1575 as being 'of Kingston Seymour'. The College of Heralds confirmed his coat of arms in 1559. He married Elizabeth Wake, daughter of Richard Wake of Northamptonshire, and they had two sons, John and Thomas. Thomas Bulbeck is described as being 'of Clevedon' so the family evidently persisted in this area for another generation at least, although there are no further surviving records of them in Clevedon documents.

In 1630, the Wake family, who had been Lords of the Manor of Clevedon since 1459, sold the Manor. In order to assess what they had to sell, Baldwin Wake's widow, Elizabeth, had a survey of the rentals and income and so forth. This was begun in 1629 and completed in 1630. The new owners of the Manor of Clevedon were the Digbys, Earls of Bristol.

In the Survey of 1630 the house heading the list of all the Clevedon farm holdings is Hide Hall. It is leased for three lives to Edward Tyson aged fifty, who holds 120 acres of land with 'a verie faire house well situated'. The yearly value is £10/8/4d.

Edward Tyson was the first of three men of that name from the same family. He came originally from Cumberland, settling in Bristol as a merchant and then buying leases in Clevedon for both Hide Hall Farm and two smaller farms called Smith's and Roe's.

This first Edward left a good inheritance to his son, of the same name, who was to be Sheriff, Alderman and, eventually, in 1659 and 1660, Mayor of Bristol. He was also Colonel of the Train-Bands of the City with 300 men armed with muskets and pikes. During his time as mayor he put down a rebellion among the Bristol apprentices at the time of the Protectorate.

His grandson was Doctor Edward Tyson, born in Clevedon in 1650, whose premier claim to fame is his pioneering research into the similarity between the skeleton and form of apes and man. He could be said to be the father of comparative anatomy. He was also a physician, the man who first introduced women into

Bethlehem Hospital as nurses and set up an out-patients' clinic there for former patients to assist them in adjusting to life outside the hospital. He was elected a Fellow of the Royal Society in 1679.

In 1652, a fragment of a second surviving Survey of Clevedon shows Edward Tyson crossed out as owner of Hide Hall and the name of a new owner written in, Thomas Knight, the son of Sir John Knight. Sir John was a prominent Member of Parliament and foremost in promoting many policies to do with the expansion of trade in England. He was Mayor of Bristol from 1663 to 1664. He also held Dowlais Farm.

Judging from a letter written by Thomas Knight to Lord Digby in 1674, there were problems with selling the farm lease to the next occupant:

> Bristoll the 7th December 1694
> Right Noble
> I had the honour to receive your Lordshippe of the 21 ult whereby your Honour is pleased to give me the change of the lives gratis, which I acknowledge as a mark of your Lordships favour, and shall look upon it as an earnest to engage me most firmly to your Lordships service which I shall always endeavour to promote to the utmost of my power, especially in those perticulars mencioned in your letter, but at the same time I must needs acquaint your Lordship of the extreame difficulty of getting purchasers in that place, by reason of the ill neighbourhood of Roger Stone and John Bullock whoe are very troublesome and vexatious to all around about them; I have for some years past bin endeavouring to sell Highdall but cannot by any means doe it for the reason above, nor should I have

got any chapman [buyer] for this; but that it lies a good distance from the concerns of those men.

I could not speak with my chapman to know the names of the lives he would he would put in till yesterday which was the reason I did not answer sooner, but now I have sent your Lordship the names of the purchaser and of the lives on which the lease is to determine, (viz) the lease must be granted to Edward Godwin of Wraxall in the County of Somersett, yeoman, and determinable on the lives of Martha Godwin his daughter aged about 5 yeares and of Mary Godwin his wife aged about 35 yeares and of himselfe whoe is aged about 40 years and he desires the lives may be named in the lease in the same order as above.

When my father purchased the tenement there was an old ruinous house upon it which by your Lordships leave hath since been suffered to goe quite to decay soe that the same is now a roofless tenement, of which your Lordships Stuard must take notice in making the lease and I shall be ready to deliver up the old lease when required by your Lordship whoe am

Right Noble

Your Lodships most Obleged

Humble servant

My Mother desired to have her humble service presented to your Lodship and Honoured Countess, etc.

Here some explanation of the mention of 'change of the lives' might clarify what was going on. Thomas had taken out what was known as a three-life lease on Hide Hall Farm. This meant that he and his two sisters were listed as the lives during which the lease would run. He would pay a large premium for the lease and a low yearly rent while the three people listed lived. When one of them died, the main lessee would be offered the chance to name a new person as a 'life', usually paying a charge for that.

It seems that Roger Stone and John Bullock had such bad reputations as neighbours that Mr Knight experienced the utmost difficulty in finding a buyer. As he says, he had to go as far afield as Wraxall to find someone who really had no idea what he was getting into. One feels sorry for poor Mr Godwin.

Both Stone and Bullock were at this time owners of several farms in Clevedon, setting in motion a new form of agriculture in which the land could be induced to crop more often and increase the yield on investments in farms. The general policy they followed was to allow the farmhouse to become uninhabitable through neglect so that rent was not charged on the house.

From what Thomas Knight says, it seems that the house at Hide Hall was a ruin when his father, Sir John Knight, purchased it. By 1694, it was completely without a roof. It appears that Mr Godwin rebuilt the house, the west end of the present building being the oldest remaining portion of the original house.

In 1730, Reuben Hollyman of Wraxall bought Hide Hall together with Dale's Farm, a smallholding in Old Street. The two farms with 97 acres of land were tenanted by Jane Pomeroy. There were two large closes of land called Tysons where the tenant was Robert Bryant. These closes were opposite Dowlais farm, off Lower Strode Road. As Robert Bryant was working the tide mill on the sea wall at this time, he would have found these fields conveniently placed.

The rent paid by Mr Hollyman was to be £110 a year, which would vary according to what he used the land for, whether it was to be pasture or arable land. There was a specification that any dung, soil, hay or straw produced was to be used on the farm, which would seem to indicate that the previous lessee had been selling this off, rather than looking after the land. Wood for repairs to the house was allowed to be cut, as well as firewood. Reuben Hollyman eventually succeeded his cousin Oswald as agent for the Clevedon Court Estate.

The Poor Rates list several different tenants during the 1760s, none of whom lasted long. In the late 18th century, however, Thomas Hollyman had Hide Hall and Dales, and his widow Elizabeth continued to hold the farms herself.

Thomas Hollyman's oldest son, Charles, was the next to take over Hide Hall. Judging by a report in the *Bristol Mirror*, 7 September, 1822, he seems to have been a rather troublesome character. I sum this up here:

Mrs Malbon and friends, among them a Captain Lawrence RN, returned from a walk to the seaside to find Charles Hollyman and Mr Kiddell looking at the front of her house. She thought they were assessing for the window tax and asked if they needed to see the interior as well. Hollyman was insolent and stepped across the fence into the flowerbeds, at which Captain Lawrence asked him not to spoil the flowers.

The Captain had been shooting at seagulls and was carrying a loaded gun, but restrained himself when Hollyman asked him for his certificate, exchanged words and struck the Captain across the face.

The point was made that the Captain was not out to gain excessive money for damages, merely that he wanted to make an example of Hollyman. Hollyman received a 5/- fine and he sincerely apologised.

This was by no means the last time that Charles Hollyman hit the headlines. In August 1825, he brought an action against a fellow churchwarden, Mr Cook: Cook struck him in the face at a churchwarden's dinner from 3pm to 11pm! In October 1828, it was revealed that he did not seem to employ reputable carters:

> On Friday at Failand Inn a servant of Mr Charles Hollyman of Clevedon was driving a waggon while drunk, and hit the Weston super Mare coach. He was fined £2/10/0d and the owners of the coach were recommended to sue for damages.

Sadly, his next mention in the local press was when he sold the farm. The transcript of the advertisement for sale is fascinating, showing the stock he had and the way in which the house was furnished:

> To be sold at Clevedon, farming stock and household furniture of Mr Charles Hollyman of Highdale Farm, Clevedon. Declining farming business.
> 14 prime young dairy cows, some near calving, 4 2-yr old heifers in calf capital 2-yr old bull a Hereford, 6 2-yr old steers, 6 weaning calves, a capital cart horse, 2 capital cart mares, one rising 4-yrs old, 1 hacking mare in foal, 1 hacking horse fit for riding or harness, 1 cart colt rising 2 yrs, 1 sow in farrow, 4 fat pigs, a Cobourg cart and harness, a quantity of haum, 50 sacks prime potatoes in lots, a capital potato washer, 2 waggons, 1 broad wheel putt with iron axles, 1 broad wheel cart, 1 narrow wheel cart, a capital field roller, pair drags, pair harrows, iron plough, 1 other field plough, 2 field drugs, 3 sets breech harness nearly new, 4 sets trace harness, 1 set

double plough harness, yokes, bows and chains, chaff box, ladders and hay knives, winnowing fan and sieve, wheelbarrow together with a large assortment of husbandry implements. Dairy utensils, 5 milk-leads, 3 cheese presses, 2 cheese tubs, barrel and tub churns, trendles, milk-pails,, tins, vats, cheese bowl and sieve, butter scales, prints etc etc.

Household items

Excellent carved mahogany four poster bed, and tent bedsteads, with chintz and dimity furnishing, stump and cross bedsteads, 4 prime goosefeather beds, 4 milpuff beds, counterpanes, quilts, blankets, mahogany commode and other chests of drawers, mahogany and painted deal dressing tables, mahogany and deal bason stands with basons and ewers, painted deal night tables, swing mirrors, bedside carpets, set of mahogany dining tables on pillars and claws, mahogany Pembroke and card tables, mahogany bureau, sofa with chintz covering, set of mahogany chairs with hair seats and brass nails nearly new, a larges Brussels carpet, a large Kidderminster carpet, an eight-day clock in a mahogany case, 3 sets of handsome china, a large assortment of blue and white earthenware, decanters and rummers, wine and other glasses, a set of castors with stand, parlour fender and fireirons, mahogany tea caddie, mahogany tea and other trays, a barometer, a telescope, double-barrelled gun with percussion lock, single-barrelled gun, a hackney side-saddle and bridles, alarum, beams and scales, kitchen tables and chairs, washing and other tubs, buckets, pails, pots etc.

Double roller cider press, with hair cloths complete, together with a large assortment of empty casks in good condition. (*Bristol Mirror, 30 March, 1833.*)

Charles Hollyman's final appearance in the *Bristol Mercury* was in 1835, two years after he sold the farm. An inquest was held at Purnell's New Hotel in Chapel Hill in Clevedon (now the Bristol Hotel) on the body of Charles Hollyman late of Highdale Farm. Rumours were rife about the death, no-one being able, or perhaps willing, to explain the circumstances.

The body was examined by Mr Davis, surgeon of Nailsea, and three other surgeons, Hollyman being found to have suffered a blow to the head causing a fracture of the skull followed by death. How the injury was received is unknown. An answer to this mystery has never been found. I suspect that he was deeply unpopular and that someone more or less finished him off for the public good.

James Kiddell was the purchaser of Hide Hall in 1833, taking on 71 acres of land and employing two men. He and his wife Mary remained there until he retired in 1865 aged 53. He had by then invested in property, buying two houses in Chapel Hill and Copse Lodge in Copse Road. He and Mary lived in Old Street, in a cottage with an orchard that once stood near the Medical centre, supporting themselves with the rents of their other houses.

The sale of stock from the farm in October 1864 included all the fat stock, dairy cows, grass, corn and implements. There followed a complete clearance in March 1865, comprising one prime young dairy cow, one cob horse six years old good to ride or drive. Thirty down ewes, some with lambs and the others lambing down, five tons of hay, a narrow-wheel waggon, hay-making machine, winnowing machine, field roller, sheep troughs, chaff cutter, hay knives, pikes and rakes. Also listed were the usual cider casks as well as all the dairy equipment. Odds and ends of household furniture were sold off too. There was 1,300 gallons of prime new cider in lots to finish the sale.

It is interesting at this point to note that the present Cottage Hospital old building was formerly a barn standing in the second barnyard of Hide Hall. The 1865 dispensary building, since replaced, was built there in 1865 following the conversion of the barn to a hospital in 1875.

The next farmer to take Hide Hall was James Stuckey from Kingston Seymour, a member of a large and widespread family of farmers and livery stable keepers. In 1861, he was living in Brunswick House on The Beach, working from there as a farmer of 43 acres with the help of one man. Brunswick House was run by his wife Elizabeth as a lodging house. They had at that time seven growing children, so Elizabeth evidently had no fear of hard work! In Kelly's Directory of 1866, Highdale Farm was also advertised as a lodging house, so they each had their own business to run. Five of their children still lived at home at Hide Hall, so his wife Elizabeth still had a lot to do. There were no servants living with them at Hide Hall, though James employed one man to work the 50 acres he took on with this farm.

In 1872, James sold Hide Hall and moved to Beach Villa on The Beach where he ran horse-drawn taxi cabs called flys. His second wife, Mary Ann, managed the house as a lodging house.

The farm sale gives a good picture of what sort of farming he practised. The advertisement in January 1872 lists

> five dairy cows in calf and a barren heifer, two
> yearling steers, yearling heifer, twenty ewes in lamb,
> fourteen fat sheep, sow and twelve pigs, sow and
> eleven pigs, four store pigs.

The list of implements and equipment is comprehensive and indicates an even balance between farming for milk, cheese, pork and wool.

Sheep rack, sheep trough, haymaking machine by Frost, winnowing machine, bouting plough, wood and stone pig troughs, single screw cider press, double roll apple mill, 10 hair cloths, tubs, two water casks, two single barrel guns, barrel churn, pump churn, double box cheese press and leads, two milk leads, cheese tub, cheese vats and followers, scales, trendles and milk pails, meat salter, bacon rack, plate rack etc.

Also, about twelve tons of English hay and fourteen acres of grass keep to the 24th of March next, 300 gallons of new cider, in convenient lots, 12 empty casks, pipes, herefords and hogsheads, cider horsing etc.

The cows are young and good milkers, the hay of prime quality and to be consumed on the premises, the grass land dry, healthy and well sheltered.

Some of the terms used above are unfamiliar now. A bouting plough is one used for making deep furrows for the planting of turnips. The hair cloths would have been used to wrap the apple pulp before the pulp was pressed. In cheese making, a follower is the piece of wood laid on top of the curd before pressing. A trendle is a shallow wooden bowl used in dairying. The size of a hereford barrel defeats me, but cider horsing would be the wooden frame that supported cider barrels when full.

The buyer of Hide Hall in 1872 did not have far to move. Bristol-born William Bryant had been farming in Clevedon in Old Church Road at Myrtle Farm, otherwise known as Coleridge Cottage, since 1858. His daughter and only child, Kate, was born in

Clevedon and his wife Mary was from Yatton. William John Bryant has left his mark at the farm: if you see boundary stones near the footpath from Christchurch down the hill past the farmhouse, they will be marked WJB and dated, as far as I recall, 1888.

William Bryant described himself as a cowkeeper in Kelly's Directory in 1875, but as a farmer in the 1881 Census. He farmed 55 acres with four labourers, living at the farm with his wife, daughter, sister Hannah, a house servant and two farm servants. Sadly, his wife predeceased him in the middle of the 1880s, not surprisingly as she was twelve years older. Kate Bryant farmed with her father until he died in 1890 and then continued at Hide Hall, marrying Ernest Brake in 1894. It was perhaps at that point that the farm was again sold.

Some of the fields leased with the farm were turned over to property development at this time. One of the fields became Highdale Avenue, where many of the houses were built by the Shopland family in 1895 and 1896. In his memoir, *Manifold Memories*, Mr Edmund Shopland relates how he gathered enough money working in his spare time to build a pair of houses in Highdale Avenue, his father supplying him with bricks and tiles in the last years of the family's brickworks in Kenn Road. The date, 1896, can still be seen on the side of the houses by the rough track up to Hide Hall Farm. By 1902, thirteen houses had been built there. More would follow as the old quarry at the west end of the Avenue was cut through into Chapel Hill.

The next farmer was William Callow who had certainly moved to Hide Hall in 1897, listed in that year's Directory. He and his second wife, Elizabeth Locke of Nailsea, had one child, Robert, born in Clevedon in 1891. Mrs Callow was named after her mother, Elizabeth Locke, who lived with the couple on her own income, aged seventy-one.

In 1901, the Census shows that William Callow was in the Cottage Hospital at Clevedon, while Elizabeth, their son and her mother stayed at the farm. Little else can be discovered excepting that William died on 13 March 1902, having shot himself in a state of exhaustion and worry. He had spent some time in the Cottage Hospital again and his wife said he had suffered badly from influenza for the previous seven or eight winters. As well as Hide Hall, he had to decide to take the farm at the Cross Tree at Walton in Gordano and was worrying about whether he had done the right thing in taking on a second enterprise.

His widow, Elizabeth, stayed on at the farm and was still listed in the Clevedon Directory for 1906, but five years later the Marshall family was at the farm. Plate 12 shows the farmhouse around 1900.

Plate 12: Hide Hall c1900

John Marshall and his wife, Ellen Sophia, were in their late twenties when the 1911 Census was taken. They had been married only three years. There were eight rooms in the farmhouse, of which they occupied six, letting two rooms to Alice Lewis, a widow aged seventy four who made an income from sewing.

By the time John Marshall took Hide Hall, the fields comprised about twenty-three-and-a-half-acres, all used for pasture. Whereas anciently a complex of fields called Hyde had belonged to the farm, these had all been incorporated in other leases when the lessees changed, or had been used for building development. The Hyde complex stretched from the farmhouse south across Old Street to the other side of the road and a little way westwards from there. John Marshall's fields more or less extended from the end of Meadow Road towards the east.

Following the Great War, there was a financial crisis in Britain during which many large estate and country houses were sold off. Rents had fallen away to such an extent that the owners could no longer afford to maintain their previous lifestyles.

The Clevedon Court Estate held two sales during 1919, the first comprising eleven farmhouses and land, the second sixty-four cottages and land. The *Clevedon Mercury* reported the wish of Sir Edmund Elton that, where possible, the houses should be purchased by the tenants, not by others wishing to make a profit from selling them on afterwards. The sale was set in motion from a desire that the tenants should benefit from the need of the Elton family to sell some of their properties, and to further building development, which would certainly increase in the town.

One of the farms sold off was Hide Hall, the particulars in the catalogue for the first sale being:

Lot 11

The desirable and exceptionally well-situated farm holding known as Highdale Farm, comprising farmhouse, outbuildings, alluvial and upland pastures containing a total area of 23 acres 2 roods 14 perches more particularly described as follows:

No. on 1903 OS Map Description State Area

366 Part of Court Farm Pasture 2.096

371 Part of Court Farm Pasture 2.782

372 Lady Croft Pasture 0.923

373(part) Lady Croft Pasture 0.906

379 Lady Croft Pasture 2.446

380 The Acre Pasture 1.031

381(part) Part of half acre, north of railway Pasture 0.037

381(part) Well Paddock and part of half acre south of railway

Pasture 2.100

388(part) Durbin's 5 Acres north of railway Pasture 1.125

388(part) Durbin's 5 Acres south of railway Pasture 3.750

389(part) Powell's 8 acres north of railway Pasture 2.162

389(part) Powell's 8 acres south of railway Pasture 3.263

402 Dwelling house, outbuildings etc - 0.931

403(part) Strip for access to back of lane etc - 0.038

Acreage 23.590

The farmhouse, which is built of stone and stuccoed and tiled, contains lobby, kitchen with cupboard under stairs, larder, 2 sitting rooms, pantry, cellar, storeroom, dairy, cider cellar, coal house, w.c., covered yard and lean-to woodshed, above are 6 bedrooms, boxroom and w.c. with flush cistern. There is a good fruit and vegetable garden in front of house.

The drainage is connected to the public sewer.

Company's water and gas are laid on.

The outbuildings include cart house, loose house with loft over, 2-stall stable, 2 calves' houses, boiler house and wood sheds, cow house with ties for 10 cattle and root house adjoining, 2 pigsties all stone and tiled. The farmhouse is within the town of Clevedon, being only about quarter mile from Clevedon Station.

The timber and tiled cow-house with 12 ties, timber and galvanized cow-house with ties for 8 cattle, loose house and cart shed, trap-house and tool-house, lean-to fowl's house all timber and galvanized, part roof of paved back let, are the property of the Tenant.

This lot is let to Mr John Marshall at a total rent of £130 per annum, the rent being apportioned to this lot being £89.

Timber £80 Commuted Tithe £7/9/7d.

John Marshall could not afford the lot himself, but his father, Isaac Weaver Marshall (who ran the West End Dairy in Clevedon), bought Hide Hall for £2,080. In 1922, Isaac W Marshall sold off all of the fields: 389 to John Shopland; 379, 380, 2 parts of 381 and 2 parts of 388 to William Henry Hill; 366, 371, 372 and part 373 to Charles Shopland. Parts of this land were later developed as part of Teignmouth Road, and much of it now lies under Beaconsfield Road.

All that he retained was 402, the plot on which the house stood. In 1923, John Marshall moved from Hide Hall to Wrangle Farm, formerly in Moor Lane but since demolished. His parents moved to Walton Road and his brother, George Marshall, took over their West End Dairy. Isaac died in 1926 and then his widow, Mrs Mercy Marshall, moved to Highdale Farm.

Plate 13 shows the house with Polly Barnes delivering milk in the 1920s. She and her business partner, Miss Robertson, set up a dairy in Station Road in 1923.

When the 1939 England and Wales Register was taken at the beginning of the Second World War, Hide Hall was still in the hands of the Marshall family. John, by then a widower and a dairy farmer, was living there with his younger sister Angel.

Plate 13: Hide Hall, Polly Barnes

The history of this farm covers over 700 years, through plague, civil unrest, dereliction, attacks from neighbours and triumphant rebuilding. For many years the farmhouse was used by

Mrs Cooke, who ran boarding kennels there. The house had once again begun to fall into ruin. In the 1970s, it was sold to Tony and Nan Williams, who made an excellent job of restoring the old house. The final photograph of Hide Hall was taken in 1975 before this panelling from an upstairs room was moved downstairs during restoration work and preserved by Tony and Nan. Without people like them we would lose much of our heritage.

Plate 14: Hide Hall panelled room upstairs c1976

Chapter 7

Mr Fowler's Plot:
Marine House, Marine Villas, York Hotel, Pier Mews

George Fowler bought a large plot at the west end of Hill Road in 1827. By 1830 he had built a shop on this land with an attached house, two semi-detached villas in their own gardens, and a coach house and stables with garden. He employed Bristol architects Foster and Okely, the designers of West Mall and Caledonia Place in Clifton, Bristol. It seems that he would have been in his mid-twenties at this time, though it is hard to find any information about him. The *Bristol Mercury* tells us that he died in 1855 after years of suffering aged only fifty-two. His daughter Rosa married in 1853 at St Andrew's Church, Clevedon, and he is recorded in the Register there as a gentleman. He was originally a victualler.

Dealing with his buildings, I shall start with the shop at 36 Hill Road, then follow that with Marine Villas, the York Hotel and the stables, moving towards the sea from the inland end of the plot.

Marine House

The shop is called Marine House, which I believe to be among the earliest purpose-built shops in Clevedon, if not the earliest: it is certainly the most beautiful. The shop stands in a commanding position on the corner of Copse Road and Hill Road facing almost east. Early visitors to the town would have discovered that it stocked almost everything they required in the way of stationery, medicines and newspapers.

The first reliable record for Clevedon in the early 19th century is a survey made in 1830. In this survey, the shop is occupied by Charles Stone, a grocer who continued there until 1834. In 1832, Mr Fowler advertised his entire Clevedon properties for sale and the shop was at that time being used as the Post Office. The annual rent in that year was £35. Nothing seems to have come of the attempt to sell and Mr Stone stayed put. In 1835, the property was taken by Henry Collis, who stayed into the late 1830s.

Plate 15: Clevedon, from the Park Hill, 1866. The curving corner shop and two buildings to the right are on Mr Fowler's plot

In 1841, the shop and house adjoining was sold to William Ransford. He had been resident in Clevedon for some years, having retired here from Frampton Cotterell in Gloucestershire where he owned a hat-making factory. He bought the premises for his son Samuel, a druggist, as chemists were called at that time.

Samuel Ransford had previously purchased a business in Bristol, Ferris and Score, which was established in 1837. This is why 'Established 1837' used to be painted on the shop frontage, above the windows. The shop itself was actually older than that!

In 1847, Samuel ran a circulating library and had a reading room at the shop, where

The morning papers of the day are now upon the table by half past eleven am, the Proprietor having lately made arrangements with the Great Western Railway Company so as to enable him to obtain them thus early, for the convenience of his Subscribers.

The shop was a stationery shop as well as a chemist's outlet. Visitors staying in the lodging houses and the hotels – there were two in Hill Road at this time – were keen to keep abreast of the latest news. The Library there could be used for £1/1s a year, or the Library and Reading Room for £1/10s a year. The lowest charge was for weekly use, when the Library cost a shilling and sixpence, or both facilities could be used for three shillings.

Two years later, he advertised that he had in stock

Concentrated essence or aroma of Jamaica ginger. Concentrated essence of chamomiles and Jamaica ginger. Concentrated or fluid extract of Sarsaparilla, containing all the medical properties of the root. Aromatic tincture of myrrh and borax, for the teeth and gums; also, camphorated pearl dentifrice.

As well as the above, he lists a staggering array of treatments and spices, candles, stationery, teas and coffees, chocolate, cigars and fancy snuffs, as well as perfumes, the delightfully named scouring drops, fumigating papers, marking ink for laundry, glue for china, enema apparatus, fish sauce, pickles and leeches.

By 1866, Samuel Ransford had amassed an impressive property portfolio in Clevedon, seven houses in Hill Road, one in Park Road and three in Copse Road. He retired in his fifties and lived in Champion House in Hill Road.

Mr Ransford continued to run the shop until the early 1860s when Henry Chapman leased the shop from him. He was also a chemist hailing originally from Banwell and was assisted in the shop by his son, William. They had been working in Clifton previously. He employed two young ladies as stationery assistants. Chapman expanded the range of stationery items, selling sheet music, religious tracts, photographic albums, artists' materials of all kinds, and toys and games. He offered walnut and leather goods, fancy items, jet goods, ivory brooches, other jewellery, maps, purses, walking sticks, flutes, musical boxes, and more besides.

By this time there were many more lodging houses in Clevedon than there had been when the shop first opened. With the larger clientele from visitors, there was an excellent market for guide books and photographic views. Henry Chapman led the field here, publishing an excellent guide book to Clevedon and the surrounding area in 1864, as well as a collection of views of Clevedon, Cheddar and the neighbourhood at only one shilling. His guide book was republished in a second edition in 1868 and the text formed the basis for several later guide books for our town. He also stocked Clevedon Lavender Water, very popular with ladies.

Sadly, Mr Chapman passed away in 1878 at the early age of fifty-one. By this time, Samuel's son William was old enough to take over the shop. His younger brother, Arthur Harwood Ransford, took responsibility for the stationery business and reading rooms, which thrived under his competent direction. He not only sold sheet music but hired and sold pianos, a very popular instrument in the days before other forms of home entertainment entered the field.

The two brothers worked on into the late 1880s when William seems to have retired from the shop. The chemist's side of the business was then run for three or four years by Alfred Orme from Macclesfield in Cheshire, then briefly by James Keeble, who moved on to Crewkerne, and then by Henry J Hart, again for three or four years.

Plate 16: Marks the Chemist in the late 1890s

Consistency was re-established with the coming of Frederick Marks, whose family would keep the shop until the 1980s. He was born in Clevedon in 1868 at the opposite end of Hill Road, in Prospect House facing Christ Church. His father was William Marks, who had moved to Clevedon in the 1860s to buy the bakery business at Prospect House. It expanded beyond recognition under his ownership to include refreshment rooms as well as the shop there.

Frederick Marks bought Marine House in 1901 and moved to Clevedon from Barnstaple where he had been running his own business. His first advertisement in Clevedon lists him as

Plate 17: Ursula Kenway 'F Marks (late Hart), Dispensing Chemist.' He made aerated waters on the premises and sold many kinds of mineral waters too, including Vichy, Apenta and Janos. He kept a large variety of photographic goods in stock, and there was a dark room available for the use of amateurs. The emphasis, no longer on patent medicines, had moved to more general merchandise.

Plate 18: Ursula Kenway in Marks Dispensing Chemist

By the 1920s, Frederick could develop and print photographs in 24 hours. He was the maker of 'Velvine' cream and soap and sold the original Clevedon Violet Perfume. This perfume became popular when the Clevedon Violet was bred by a local market gardener, George Lee, who used to send the flowers to Queen Victoria, having gained her permission to name the hybrid after her. The flowers were sent out in hampers to Covent Garden from the Clevedon Railway Station near the Triangle, and were said to fill the air with their scent. As well as perfume, talcum powder was also a good line. The bottle labels and boxes were still in the basement when the business changed hands in the 1980s!

The Marks family stayed on at Marine House, trading as Marks and Son in the 1950s, and then as B. Marks in the 1960s. The emphasis remained on photographic stock, with cine film being added to the lines in the early 1950s. By then, cosmetics and perfumes were evidently doing well and Marks were sole agents (in Clevedon at least) for Elizabeth Arden. By 1968, home wine making was being taken up and the shop carried a comprehensive stock of materials for this newly popular hobby.

Also during the 1950s the adjoining shop at number 38, formerly the Library and Reading Rooms, was transformed into Marks and House Electrical and Radio Engineers, selling Philips radios and Murphy radios and hiring out battery and electric televisions.

In the 1980s, the shop was sold and renovated to continue to be run as a chemist's shop for a few more years. Now, it is The Cellar, a wine bar serving food, with bed and breakfast rooms also on offer.

The old interior of the shop, listed Grade 2, remains much as it was, with the quarter-circle counter moved to a different part of the old shop area, but carefully retained. The shop fittings are all original dating back to the 1820s and 1830s, with beautiful wooden drawers with hand painted and stencilled labels.

Marine Villas

Moving along the plot towards the sea, the next building is a pair of villas originally called Marine Villas and now named Whitsom Lodge and The Lookout. This seems to have been the first building on the plot. I'll refer to them by these names, as it is less confusing. Clevedon people tend to refer to the houses as, 'the one with the mermaid and the one with the life belt' – these individual additions were made in the 1960s. Dick Taylor added the mermaid to his house with the help of a sculptor from the Royal West of England College of Art. The neighbours felt that it would be a nice thing to balance this with the lifebelt – this all works very well!

The pair of villas mirror each other, laid out with two rooms on each floor. There are four floors in all as the houses are built into a steep slope; the basement level is only apparent from the back of the villas. The kitchen, water closet and china pantry referred to in the 1832 sale particulars would have been on the basement floor, with servants' sleeping quarters in the attic. Water was obtained from a well situated behind what is now called Marine Hill House, shared with the other premises on the plot.

From the Rate books, it seems that Mr Fowler retained the use of The Lookout for himself. Whitsom Lodge was let to a Thomas Powell who ran a boarding school there for boys, or as they were known in those days, 'young gentlemen'.

Mr Powell moved away and the house continued as a boarding school under the management of the Armstrong sisters, Mary, Lucy and Sophia, who were all in their twenties. They advertised the school to let in 1839, but in the 1841 Census, they are still there, with ten young ladies resident as pupils, ranging in ages from six to seventeen. Two servants made a total of fifteen ladies living at the house. There were five generous bedrooms, a drawing room and dining room linked with a folding door, and a breakfast parlour, though the bedrooms must have been shared.

In 1843, the Misses Armstrong moved out to Stokes Croft in Bristol to different premises. In that year, Mary, the oldest sister, married. The school was carried on by Lucy and Sophia until Lucy married Matthew Lister in 1849, returning to teaching after her husband's death. Sophia looked after her widowed father until his death in 1858 after which she ran a boarding school again.

In 1851, Whitsom Lodge was taken by a peripatetic widow and her daughters, Mrs Eliza Hicks, along with Emma, Fanny,

Charlotte and Margaret. The Hicks family name has been associated with a variety of types of mills in Gloucestershire since the mid-16th century. They were long known as owners of grist mills, fulling mills and cloth mills. In the late 18th century, they became established in Eastington, eventually owning four mills there on the river Frome: Bond's Mill; Churchend Mill; Millend Mill and Meadow Mill.

They were the first in that area to use steam power, installing engines in their four mills between 1818 and 1826. Henry Hicks had become Lord of the Manor in 1806, buying a large estate and building himself a grand house in Eastington in 1815. Though this was a great venture, in 1835 he was declared bankrupt. His oldest son, John Phillimore Hicks, died in January of that year and Henry died in the June.

What remained of his estates was split between his widow Catherine, his surviving son Henry Purnell Hicks, and John Phillimore Hicks' widow, Eliza Hicks. Eliza Hicks was to be the last person to claim Manorial rights in Eastington. Eliza and her four daughters lived in France for a few years after John Hicks' death. In 1841, they were living in Cheltenham and then moved to Clevedon, where they lived in several houses in succession, the daughters eventually having a house built for themselves in Lower Linden Road.

George Fowler, the original owner of the plot, died in 1855 after years of suffering and his properties were sold. During the 1850s, occupants ranged from men in holy orders to retired admirals. In 1861, Mary Roberts, a widow, ran one of the houses as a lodging house. With sweeping views across the Mendip Hills and the Bristol Channel, the position was ideal. For several decades the houses were let for the summer. As the census was being taken in the spring, before visitors arrived, only one seems to have been occupied earlier in the year.

Fortunately it was common practice for people moving out of a house to sell off the furniture when they left and newspaper advertisements list many of the items, giving us a clear impression of the style of house contents. In 1863, Whitsom Lodge was the site of an auction of the furniture of a lady leaving the house. Among the items for sale were beds and bedding, mattresses of various kinds, mahogany furniture, tables, couches, large bookcases, card tables, carpets, rugs, fenders and china.

In 1862, The Lookout was advertised to let unfurnished at £50 a year. The furniture could be purchased by the incoming tenant if they wished. The advertisement revealed that the house had both kinds of water – as ever, this means hard water from the well and soft water from collecting rain in a cistern. This soft water was invaluable for laundry work.

The year 1882 saw the sale of the furniture left behind by the Misses Tothill, three young sisters who ran Whitsom Lodge as a boarding house. Adelaide, Emily and Sarah Tothill were aged between nineteen and sixteen, their affairs cared for by Trustees after their father's death in 1879. They seem shockingly young to be running a venture like a boarding house. It seems that the sisters went to Canada in 1886 and continued to live there for the rest of their lives.

In 1891, Whitsom Lodge was once again a small boarding school managed by John Bailey, his wife and their two daughters. Stella Bailey was the music teacher and Florence a governess. There were five boys aged from eight to fifteen boarding with the Baileys. As one of the neighbours was also a governess, it seems likely that she worked at the school too.

By that time, the census had at last caught up with the occupants of The Lookout, Mr Frederick Mills, a retired master mariner and his family from Bristol. He had worked from Hackney and Westbury-on-Trym in previous census returns. Clevedon was always popular with retired people who wanted to live in a quiet place.

From here on there is little to say about the two houses. Whitsom Lodge is still a single dwelling. The Lookout has been divided into flats for some years now. The house names seem to have appeared at different dates, Whitsom Lodge being named in 1911 and The Lookout in the 1920s.

With regard to the continued occurrence of boarding schools, there were a great many of these small private schools in Clevedon over the course of the 19th century because of its healthy situation and good road and rail links. During that century and into the 20th century too, many people still served abroad with the Indian Army and the East India Company. Their children would not have enjoyed a tropical climate and so were sent home to be educated.

The York Hotel, now Marine Hill House

The western part of the plot, with the land falling away steeply towards the direction of the sea, was where Mr Fowler sited a large house. The lie of the land meant that he was able to cut away soil and rock to make a flat site for extensive stabling below the sight-line of the hotel guests, leaving them with an open view down the Channel and across to Wales. The rock would have been used in his building work, any surplus generally finding an outlet in road making.

This was the last building he put up on the plot and was not listed in the Survey in 1830. However, it had been built by 1832 when Mr Fowler tried to sell all of his Clevedon properties. He seems to have found no takers despite the excellent situation and extensive views across the Bristol Channel and to the Mendip Hills. In the description of the sale, Lot 1 is described thus:

> A Newly-built, Substantial, and Convenient Dwelling House opposite the Hotel, consisting of fourteen excellent Bed-rooms, nine Sitting-rooms, Kitchen, Servants' hall, Cellars and other necessary and convenient Offices and Garden-ground.

Frontage next the road, 238 feet, average depth, 109 feet.

This Lot is well adapted for an Hotel or Boarding-House, and will be sold subject to a Ground-Rent of £15 per annum.

The hotel opposite the dwelling house was the Royal Hotel, the first hotel to be built in Clevedon in 1826. Its site is now part of the Friary and Friary Close complex.

In 1834, the rate was raised to allow for the extra stabling Mr Fowler had added, as well as the coach houses. Failing to sell the house, Mr Fowler took decisive action and made it into a hotel, the York Hotel. (This is the building now known as Marine Hill House, which, previous to that, was a convent with attached land and a school.)

This advertisement appeared in the *Bristol Mirror*, 23 April 1836:

York House and Family Hotel.
Proprietor G Fowler. Now able to supply wines. License has been granted. Mr Fowler has also built spacious Coffee Rooms with entrance separate from the Hotel.
Good lock-up coach houses and superior stabling.

A letter sent in September 1843 by William Noel to his wife had this to say, mentioning the coffee room:

…I got to this Hotel about 6 o'clock. The Evening was delicious and such a glorious Sunset, the Bristol Channel was crimson for miles...There is something very exhilarating in this place, notwithstanding the muddiness of the water. The Coffee Room is very spacious and with Bow Windows. As the frame opens to a boundless view of the Channel and this very beautiful [illegible] has enticed numerous Parties of Gay Ladies out upon the Rocks and some of these days I anticipate spending a few days with you here as I am certain you would like it for a short time.

Mr Noel would not have been aware that he followed a summer guest at the York Hotel who is now famous in this region in particular and in the world in general. In the summer of 1843, Isambard Kingdom Brunel, now regarded as among the greatest of Victorian engineers, stayed at the York Hotel while work continued at Bristol Docks on the launch preparations for his first large ocean-going ship, the SS Great Britain. She had her own purpose-built dock at Bristol to which she was brought back from a ships' graveyard in the Falkland Islands in 1970 and where she is now on show as an excellent visitor attraction.

The hotel was commodious, described in a lease of 1840, in which William Hollyman took it over for seven years, as having some 25 bedrooms and parlours. In a list of the fixtures was a bell board in the 'passadge' [sic] with 22 bells. (This would have kept the staff on the hop!) The Census of 1841 shows the establishment being run by the Misses Sadler and Miss Cox. The sisters looked after the inn-keeping side of the business and Miss Cox the accommodation. There were ten general servants, the youngest being Samuel Dart aged only seven.

There were seven guests staying when the Census was taken in 1841, 6th June, among them several people of independent means and a librarian and his wife.

Ten years later and earlier in the season on 30th March, the 1851 Census gives the information that Elizabeth and Mary Ann Offer were running the hotel between them. Elizabeth was Mary Ann's aunt. They employed a cook, kitchen maid and chamber maid living in, together with a house maid, bar maid, the ubiquitous 'boots', a lady's maid and a livery servant. The livery servant, Thomas Grove, would have been the one in charge of visitors' horses as well as the hotel brake which called at the station in the Triangle to collect guests arriving on the Bristol and Exeter branch line from Yatton to Clevedon. He would have been the man in charge of the stabling and coach houses on the site of what is now 9 Marine Parade.

There was keen competition between the York Hotel and its older rival, the Royal Hotel, on the opposite side of the road. Both hotels collected visitors from Yatton railway station from 1841 and, from 1847, from Clevedon Station, after the laying out of a branch from the main line at Yatton. I wonder how often there were horse brakes from both hotels at the station contesting ownership of visitors.

The Offers moved out of the hotel later in 1851 and took up residence in their new venture, the Bellevue Boarding House in Bellevue Road. The contents of the York Hotel were again put up for auction, it seems, being advertised in the *Bristol Mercury* in June 1851. The reason given was that Mrs Offer was in poor health. All furniture was to be sold, plated goods, table china, cut-glass, beer and spirit machines, a bagatelle table as well as their stocks of wine and spirits and about 300 gallons of bitter ale.

A month later, Mr Fowler announced that he would take over the running of the hotel, with Mrs Fowler supervising the domestic arrangements. He was in very poor health himself and seems always to have had very little luck in selling any of his properties. In 1853, he again advertised the York Hotel and the two Marine Villas:

> Lot 1. All that Family Hotel, known as the York Hotel, most eligibly situate near the Sea, at the fashionable watering-place of Clevedon...comprising public rooms ands suites of commodious apartments, a large refreshment and billiard room, and every

convenience for an Hotel of the most respectable class, now in full business, and in the possession of Mr George Fowler, together with the garden and pleasure ground, and extensive stabling and coach-houses adjoining. There are a well and pump with an inexhaustible supply of excellent water, on the premises.

Part of the stables and coach yard lying opposite to the public baths would afford, without detriment to the hotel, a capital site for the erection of a dwelling house or lodging house, in a most desirable position.

Lot 2. A well-built and commodious semi-detached villa and garden, near adjoining to the hotel, now also in the possession of Mr George Fowler.

Lot 3. Another villa and garden, adjoining to Lot 2, now in the occupation of Miss Ashcroft, at the reduced rent of £40 per annum.

Each of Lots 2 and 3 will have the right to use the well and pump on Lot 1, with a right of way thereto.

A Fee-farm-rent of £2 12s 6d, charged on the whole of the above property, is intended to be made payable out of Lot 1.

The Fowlers again advertised the hotel for sale in December 1854, this time with rather better luck at last. Poor Mr Fowler died in March 1855 during which month the contents of the hotel were sold off, with the added comment in the advertisement that, 'All the above hotel is now sold for a gentleman's residence'.

This is the point at which Peter Guillebaud, a Clerk in Holy Orders but without a parish, bought the hotel. He and his son-in-law, Dr Theodore Davis, made the hotel into a large family house, naming it Lea Grove. Lea was Mrs Eliza Guillebaud's maiden name. Leagrove Road now runs along the southern boundary of the plot of land occupied by much of Mr Fowler's plot. When it was first laid out in the early 1860s it was called Atlantic Terrace. The Guillebaud family came originally from France, moving to London with many other Huguenot families when Protestantism was outlawed there in the 17th century.

In 1861, Mr Guillebaud's family was large and must have filled the house comfortably, even with its 25 bedrooms and parlours. Mr Guillebaud was there, along with his widowed sister and his wife's widowed sister as well as Dr Davis and his wife, with their seven children. They had two other ladies visiting them so the servants would have had plenty to keep them busy. The house had a cook, a lady's maid, two general servants and a page. The total number of people in the house was nineteen

The stables were now called Leagrove Lodge and this was where the coachman, Moses Gould, lived with his wife and two children. His daughter was a dressmaker, his son worked as a porter, and also living with them was an errand boy, William Parkhouse. No doubt there was plenty of work for the two boys from the shops in Hill Road.

Peter Guillebaud died at Lea Grove in 1867 leaving just under £120,000, a considerable fortune at that time. The house was put up for sale and bought by Dr Davis, who continued to live there until he moved to Surrey in 1872. Dr Davis was very well thought of in Clevedon where, as well as attending on members of the Elton family at Clevedon Court and the gentry, he helped to establish and run the Dispensary for the poorer population in Clevedon. This was long before the days of the National Health Service and the patient paid the doctor for visits and for medicine. At the Dispensary, the doctors gave their services and donated medicines or sold them at cost.

In 1872, the house and garden were advertised together with stables and coach houses, with a large piece of garden ground attached, described as 'a large piece of productive garden ground, well adapted for building sites, having extensive frontages, and being free from restrictions'.

The buyer was Henry Daniel, who let the main house, Lea Grove and the garden adjoining it, to Joseph Cottle. Joseph's wife Mary ran the house as a lodging house and continued after his death in 1880. By 1883, she had moved to Garfield Villa in Albert Road and the house was let to John Harris, a lodging house keeper.

Here, a little more about Henry Daniel, the new owner of Lea Grove. He was a carpenter and builder born in Sidmouth in Devon. He built up quite a portfolio by developing the land which came with both Lea Grove and with Highcliffe House in Copse Road, which he had also purchased. In 1881, he asked the Local Board of Health whether, if he gave them enough land to make up his proposed new road, they would lay it out and adopt it. They declined because it would set an awkward precedent. The new road would eventually become Leagrove Road: the part closer to The Beach had already been developed by a Mr Locock in the 1860s, along with The Towers. Mr Daniel's plan was to follow the line of that road, then called Atlantic Terrace, through to the upper part of Copse Road.

This he did, not without an eventful time. In the Minutes of the Local Board of Health, 1st November 1882, this was the report made of his problem:

> In his report the Surveyor said that it was no doubt well known to the members of the Board; that a considerable part of two villas fell down in Atlantic Terrace on 24th October. No doubt the heavy rains contributed to the cause but, "... in some parts of the building the character of the work & workmanship is bad in the extreme & not at all likely to resist a violent storm, either of wind or rain, ... the builders should not be allowed under any circumstances whatsoever to mix loam with lime for building

purposes. They argue that loam or 'Mold' as they call it, makes the mortar tough & so it dries [but it] also destroys the cohesive nature of the lime & therefore makes it useless".

After this, work was carried out to a higher standard, but the road was renamed probably, in part, because it became a local byword that the houses fell down in the rain! From the day Mr Daniel completed the road, and when the Local Board of Health adopted it in 1886, it was named Leagrove Road.

Incidentally, from the Rates taken in 1891, Mr Daniel owned 16 houses in both Leagrove Road and in Marine Parade facing the Pier. He himself lived in a cottage at West End, Old Church Road, which he rented from the Clevedon Court Estate!

Returning to the story of Lea Grove itself, John Harris had already been renting stables which belonged to the house, trading as a fly (horse-drawn taxi) driver and offering livery stables there from 1881. With his wife and family he lived at Perth Villa in Marine Parade where they ran a lodging house. They were keen to take up the challenge offered by premises as large as Lea Grove and became the tenants from 1883 onwards.

By 1889, Kelly's Directory listed Mr Harris at Beach Villa. He had moved away from Lea Grove at which point the house was taken over by an order of French nuns. There were six of them who had arrived at Bristol in 1887. They had established a school at Mortimer House in Wellington Terrace, but had outgrown the house there, hence the move to Marine Hill.

As Michael Huscroft relates in his excellent guide, *The Parish and Church of the Immaculate Conception, Clevedon*, the nuns started a private school at Lea Grove, renamed St Gabriel's, also taking paying guests. Postulants were arriving there too, women who wanted to join the order. A boarding school was opened which, by 1902, was taking in deprived and orphaned children from London. By 1891, the Census showed that there were

10 nuns resident and 23 children. In 1912, the nuns left, moving to Harrow-on-the-Hill, and the children and school were transferred to La Retraite School in Wellington Terrace.

The house stood empty at times but, by the 1920s, it was a lounge café run by Mr A and Mrs Thomas Osmond. This continued until 1928 when it again became the York Hotel under the management of Mr Gordon L Griffiths. A couple of years after that it was run by Mrs E Stafford both as the Royal York Hotel and a lounge café, until it was sold in 1936.

It was in 1936 that history repeated itself and the premises were again bought by an order of nuns. Michael Huscroft tells us that the Sisters of Mercy in Bristol were able to buy the house using the dowry of one of their order. They set up what was intended to be a holiday home for the sisters. There were four sisters in place initially who, on the advice of their bishop, began to take school pupils as boarders. This eventually continued as a day school only and the nuns took in lady boarders instead. In addition, they assisted the Franciscan friars at the Friary across the road from the house, visiting the sick and helping with religious teachings.

After the Second World War, the Catholic population of the town increased, which meant that the school could expand, utilising more buildings and being named St Anthony's School. This was an excellent private primary school with a nursery school added in 1974. The school closed in 1991 because the order of nuns had decided that they would no longer undertake private education. During its lifetime, the school earned a high reputation in the area, preparing its pupils to an excellent standard for higher education.

The nuns remained and part of the buildings became a day centre for a mental health unit, with the two bungalows, formerly schoolrooms, for families in poor circumstances or in need of a change of surroundings.

Eventually, the order sold the house and, in recent years, it has been redeveloped into flats, entering a new phase of its 180-year existence.

The Stables, now 9 Marine Parade

It was Mr Daniel who let the stables separately from Lea Grove after he purchased the buildings in 1872, the first tenant listed in the 1875 Rates being Mark Crease. By 1879, the proprietor of the livery stables and fly or horse-driven taxi service based here was John Harris. In that year, he was employing George Garrett, reported to the police for embezzling money from his master. In other words, he was accused of pocketing the fares paid by Mr Harris's clients. The case could not be proved.

Mr Harris had several trying times at the stables. In 1881, he ordered a drunk out of his yard and was abused and beaten by the fellow. PC Tilly, who was called in, was also assaulted and had considerable trouble in arresting the offender and taking him to the lock-up in Chapel Hill. At this time, the lock-up was in one of a pair of cottages standing just above the Bristol Hotel, the house nearest to the hotel. It was actually in the back garden and was generally used by the policeman's wife as a store for her mangle, as we shall discover later in this narrative!

In 1883, Mr Harris was involved in a case of horse theft when his premises were used by the thief, more or less to give a screen of respectability to the theft. The criminal had purchased a horse in Nailsea using a dud cheque. After the horse was delivered to Mr Harris's stables, the thief calmly saddled up using one of the saddles belonging to Mr Harris and rode off, never to be found.

Also, in 1883, he was instrumental in rescuing a suicide from her intended fate. He heard a cry of distress from the sea and hurried to the water's edge where, with much difficulty, he was able to drag a woman ashore. He called PC Tilly, who managed to detach the lady from a gentleman she had grabbed and took her to the house of Police Sergeant Milburn (Chapel Hill) where she was dried and put to bed by Mrs Milburn. She was respectably dressed in a black silk dress, fur-lined cloak and black hat. She proved to be a widow addicted to drink. She appeared before the Magistrates the following day and was given into the care of her friends.

John Harris lived at Perth Villa in Marine Parade in 1881. He renamed the stables, 'Pier Mews', and James Neads, a labourer, lived in the mews house with his wife and small son.

Ten years later, the Rates and Census of 1891 tell us that the stables now belonged to Albert Lewis, and that James Neads had become a cabman. His younger brother, John Neads, was lodging with James and his family, and also was a cabman. In that Census, Albert Lewis was a carriage proprietor and, in the Directory of Clevedon for 1897, he is listed as providing 'livery and bait' (stabling and food), at Marine Parade, so he could be assumed to be the Neads brothers' employer. He was also a coal merchant, running that side of his business from the West End of Old Church Road.

In 1894, Mr Lewis went out of business, owing £163/4/8d. The official receiver observed that 'This debtor, who previously a coachman, started business on his own account in 1891 as a livery stable keeper and oil and coal dealer with a capital of £135.'

His effects were sold to meet his debts, but only £67 was raised, most of which was owed in rent. Mrs Lewis ran lodgings at their house and was said to have purchased some of the furniture herself, which would mean it could not be seized to pay her husband's debts. The cause of the failure of his business was said to be 'Loss and illness of horses, bad trade, and paying too heavy a rental for the business done at the mews'.

In 1900, the Rates still list Albert Lewis at the Mews and living at the house at 7 Marine Parade. However, the Census in 1901 lists James Neads as a labourer again, living at 7a Marine Parade with his wife and three children: Annie was a dressmaker, Edward was a gardener's assistant – perhaps at the nursery gardens behind Highcliffe House, backing onto the old York Hotel land – and John Lawford Neads, the youngest, was still at school.

By 1906, there were several people listed at what was then

number 7 Marine Parade: Miss Ford, Miss Free and Mr Sweet. At 7a, where the mews were sited, were Mr and Mrs Atwell, but no trade is given. Perhaps the business was temporarily suspended or they chose not to advertise.

It may be that the stables themselves were used by James Neads' mother Louisa Neads, one of the owners of donkeys hired out for rides on The Beach. Louisa lived in Kenn Road. By this time, she had taken on a job as a donkey woman, and was to pursue this for many years after her husband's death in 1889. This was seasonal work so she'd have had to work hard for her money while the visitors were here.

The donkey people were often rather a trial to the Board, as they had to have the donkeys inspected every season for fleas and lice. There were frequent complaints that the boys left in charge of them gambled and swore while they waited for custom. There were proper stands for the donkeys, one of them below Spray Point at the bottom of Seavale Road, now marked by a brass plaque. In 1911, Louisa Neads died aged 77.

In the 1911 Directory published in the *Clevedon Mercury*, the Pier Mews was occupied by Mr and Mrs Trebble. William Henry Trebble had been born in Ireland in about 1870 and came to Clevedon as a very small child. He was nicknamed, with the mordant local sense of humour, 'Trinity', but woe betide anyone who used this to his face! He was the last of Clevedon's cab drivers to use a horse, retiring just before the last war. Derek Lilly gave me a transcript of an interview with Mr Trebble undertaken just after he retired in the mid-1930s. He gives a vivid picture of his working life:

> I've been a cabby in Clevedon for 52 years so I ought to know a bit about it. I was a child in arms when I came to Clevedon first and I've lived here all my life. I was 65 two days ago – the day the new transmitter was opened (c.1935).

As soon as I left school, I started driving a pony and trap and I've had a cab license ever since, until 6 months ago. Then my horse was thirty years old so I had to finish up – to my sorrow. I'd like to have fifty years more at cab driving…it's a rough and ready life – lazy sometimes, other times a tiring one; we used to be out to balls and parties six nights out of seven. Clevedon was a fashionable place with gentry's houses round about the district and lords and ladies staying at the big hotels.

But it wasn't only the gentry that used to come to Clevedon…On Saturday afternoons we'd get excursionists by train from Bristol, or coming by boats from South Wales. Then you'd see the beer bottles flying.

My grandfather was the Station Policeman. In those days, the policemen wore top hats – they called them drain pipes. I remember when he was just on sixty, he was on the railway station one day, and two fellows were fighting on the platform. So my Grandfather comes along and says, 'Now what's up?' One of them went for him, but my Grandfather laid him out. Then the other one came rushing up, but my Grandfather did for him too. Then he drawed his staff and said, 'Now you stop there until I let you go.' And he kept them lying on the platform until the train was due to start. Then he said, 'Now get up and get in the train and don't come to Clevedon with any more of your impudence.'

In those days there was no Police Station in Clevedon, so they used my Grandmother's washhouse as the lock-up. One day, she was in the middle of washing and the Police Sergeant - a stout old chap he was - the Police Sergeant came along with two prisoners and he said to my Grandmother, 'Come along, out with that washtub!' And out they bundled tubs and pans and buckets and everything, and I remember seeing the Sergeant pushing the mangle out as well. My Grandmother used to hand things in to the prisoners through the bars.

Of course Clevedon has changed a lot since then. I remember when it wasn't a quarter so big...no bathing lake, no playing fields, no steam laundry, nor no cinema. It's very much improved since then. It's very healthy too. People live here from 70 to 100 years old. My Grandfather was 101 when he died, and my father was 99 years and 9 months...he was an old Crimea veteran.

Well then, I'll go back to my old cabbing career. In my prime, there were about 50 cabs in Clevedon. I was the last. Motors came in and drove us off the road...But I know a way to get to Bristol quicker than the motors can. I can do it in five minutes. And I wonder how many people know how it's done. The answer to that is that the end of the Pier is in the Bristol Parish of St Stephen's, and if I want to walk from Clevedon to Bristol I can do it in five minutes by walking from one end of the Pier to the other. But now that the BBC's come to Clevedon I suppose that we're going to be nearer to Bristol than ever and Clevedon's going to be known to hundreds and thousands of people who have never been near it. But if they come to Clevedon they'll like it...I've lived here all my life and if I hadn't liked it I'd have left years ago.

William Trebble's grandfather was Charles, who came from North Petherton. He lived in the cottage I described earlier in

Chapel Hill. The cottage nearest the pub was the police station until 1888 when a new one was built in Old Church Road, since demolished to make way for Great Western Road.

And there the story of Pier Mews ends, the business having survived beyond the rest of the many mews and livery stables in Clevedon.

Plate 19: William Henry Trebble at his post, the Pier end of The Beach

Chapter 8

The Lawn School

From the time Clevedon was first developed as a resort from the 1820s onwards, there was scope for boarding schools, usually described as 'for the sons/daughters of gentlemen'. At this time, Britain had a great empire, often in countries where it was thought that British children would not flourish in their tropical climates. All over Britain, small seaside towns provided both healthy environments and good education for these children. The schools also provided employment for young ladies with no prospect of marriage and helped swell local economies. As Derek Lilly says, too, the price bracket suited the income of the clientele who were, in our case here, mainly employed by the East India Company or the armed forces.

The Lawn School was late on the scene compared to most of these establishments, but had great success in this field, lasting for some 35 years. It was founded in 1900 in Clevedon by Miss Edith Gertrude Young and Miss Winifred Wiltshier, making a modest start in one room in a house in Elton Road called Oaklands. Oaklands, long since demolished, was a large house in generous grounds owned, at that time, by Mr Ernest Wills, a member of the Bristol tobacco family. Mrs Ernest Wills was one of the patrons listed on the printed sheet used to advertise the beginning of the school. The other patrons included Sir Edmund and Lady Elton of Clevedon Court, members of the Gibbs family from Tyntesfield at Wraxall and London, and Lieutenant-General Sir William and Lady Bellairs of Clevedon. Further patrons were gentry also related to the Elton and Gibbs families.

Edith Gertrude Young was born in 1874 in London. Her father, Gerald Young, was a nephew of Dame Rhoda Elton, the wife of Sir Arthur Elton of Clevedon Court. In addition, her uncle, Charles Young, had married into a branch of the Elton family based at Whitestaunton Manor near Chard in Somerset. So, it is no wonder that Edith Young had support from Sir Edmund and Lady Elton when she started a small private school in Clevedon.

Her fellow teacher, Miss Winifred Wiltshier, was from Canterbury and had worked as a governess in Hythe, at Rock House Ladies School, near Folkestone in Kent. She was one of three governesses and three teachers there in 1901, along with a house mistress, dealing with sixteen pupils. She and Edith Young taught according to the principles of Froebel and Pestalozzi, taking children from the age of three. (Froebel invented the kindergarten system, in which children learned through constructive play. Pestalozzi evolved a new way of teaching which revolved around the child, not just the teacher.) Outdoor exercise was taken every day, and lessons were taught in enjoyable ways, cultivating imagination and observation. The fees were three guineas a term in advance, hours from 10 am until 12 noon.

Plate 20: The Lawn School, Madeira Road, 1903

By the beginning of August 1902, Miss Young and Miss Wiltshier had moved to Madeira Road taking on a limited number of children as boarders. The house they occupied there had 11 rooms, plenty of space after being in a single room in Oaklands. Plate 20 shows these premises in 1903.

The school rapidly gained an excellent reputation, taking children whose parents lived abroad in hot countries and giving them fresh air and entertaining lessons. Beginning as a kindergarten for young children, it expanded steadily to become a boarding school for young ladies and, in August 1904, the school moved to Albert Road. Initially, Miss Young and Miss Wiltshier bought Elmhurst, after a few years moving from there next door to Clevelands and adding the adjoining house Rosemont, giving them a total of 31 rooms to use as classrooms and dormitories. Interestingly, when Elmhurst was renovated in the 1980s, the attic was found still to contain some of the old iron bedsteads used at the school. Plates 21 and 22 are from an advertisement of 1905.

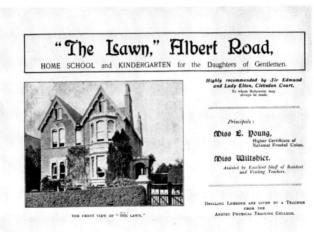

Plate 21: The Lawn School, Albert Road, 1905

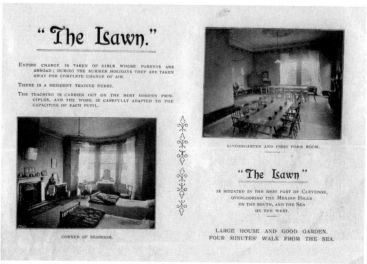

Plate 22: The Lawn School, Albert Road, 1905

In 1915, after Miss Young married, Miss Wiltshier took over the entire ownership and management of the school. She was to continue in sole charge until the mid-1930s.

Another house which became part of The Lawn School for a while was Rycote Lodge. This house had been built for Thomas Sheldon, partner in the Sheldon, Bush and Patent Shot Company of Bristol. In time, it was sold to a family called Forbes who renamed it Moraston. The Lawn School moved there during the Great War, using it largely as teaching rooms and calling it Lawnside.

The list of girls boarding at Clevelands in the 1911 Census is fascinating. Seven were born in India, one in Jamaica and another in Ireland. Betty Strachey Marriott was related to the great Bloomsbury Group writer, Lytton Strachey, whose family originally hailed from Newton St Loe near Bath. Among the occupations followed by their fathers were those of land agent, surgeon, Indian Army, school master and bank manager. There were also those of private means who enjoyed income from family money, so they were among the upper middle classes. One father, amusingly, gave his occupation as 'living on other people's means'. I take this to mean that he had income from rents on property! An advertisement in a local guide book following the Great War says severely 'For the daughters of Gentlemen only'.

Several of the girls boarding at the school were related to the Elton family, including Phyllis Kindersley and Violet Townshend, as well as Christine Hamilton, whose mother was a Kindersley. Sir Ambrose Elton's sister Kathleen had married Guy Kindersley.

To give an idea of the diversity of the pupils at the school, here is the list of people who slept the night at Clevelands and Rosemont combined as the Lawn School as recorded in the 1911 census:

Name	Age	Occupation
school staff		
Edith Gertrude Young	36	principal of school
Winifred Wiltshier	34	principal of school
Frances Gordon Stephens	24	teacher
Winifred Mary Elliott	21	teacher
Louise Guillaume	39	teacher
Ethel Mary Julian	22	teacher
Edith Madeleine Treacher	26	hospital nurse
servants		
Theodora Ann Blacker	21	cook
Annie Horler	15	kitchen maid
Winifred Mary Humphries	18	housemaid
Ethel May Quick	19	housemaid
Kate Jemima Lovell	25	housemaid

Name	Age	Place of birth
Pupils		
Eleanor Gertrude Knatchbull	16	Branscombe
Elsie Macnab	14	Itchen
Barbara Allan Macnab	12	India
Milicent Crowe	16	Ennis
Violet Mary Plowman	14	Clapham
Constance Marion Temple-Cole	14	Bath
Eileen Winifred Helen Palgrave	14	Southsea Hants
Phyllis Gertrude Kindersley	17	Assam
Violet Frances Victoria Townshend	16	Ilmington Warks
Frances Georgina Miller	16	Birmingham
Muriel Louise Anderson	17	Dublin Ireland
Olive Mary Pawsey	18	Kingston
Dorothea Wyndham Knatchbull	14	Branscombe
Beatrice Wadham Knatchbull	12	Bradford on Avon
Marjorie Isabel Edwards	13	East Grinstead
Mary Catherine Davies	11	Nainital
Kathleen Joan Hepper	12	Mussoure
Christine Mary Hamilton	9	Simla
Betty Strachey Marriott	10	Tonbridge
Phyllis Marjorie Davies	10	Mussoure
Georgina Beatrice Mary Fendall	12	Lahore
Florence Maude Hepper	13	Abbatebad
C Margaret Gabrielle Hadingham,	10	Newnham on Severn, Glos.
Number of rooms: 31		*Number of residents:* 35

In 1918, Mollie M Kaye arrived at the Lawn School to board. Her parents were well settled in India and her father, Sir Cecil Kaye, was an intelligence officer in the Indian Army. Their wider family had been associated with the Raj for many years.

Mollie became a successful author, writing many novels based in India, the best known being *Far Pavilions*, televised some years ago. She also wrote a series of detective novels.

She was happy at the school where, as well as boarders, there were enough day pupils to bring the total number of pupils to between 50 and 60. The only snag was that she and her sister Bets could be understood if they spoke to each other in Hindustani because so many of the girls spoke that language! The two girls had previously been able to communicate with each other using Hindustani without others realising what they were saying. She writes about part of her time there in the first volume of her autobiography, *The Sun In The Morning*, and here are a few of her memories of the school.

Mollie's particular friend at the school was Cynthia Hepper, a relative of the two Hepper girls listed above. Cynthia stayed at the Lawn School all year round and had discovered that Miss Wiltshier was a far more relaxed person during the carefree school holidays. By this time, Miss Young had married and left the school. Miss Wiltshier took the girls to the shore to watch the Cutty Sark sailing up the Bristol Channel, which Mollie recalled as one of the most beautiful sights she'd ever seen. Mollie also remembered a fire in the coal cellar, enthusiastically put out with the help of the entire school.

The girls were regularly taken for walks in the town to have some fresh air and a change of scene. No doubt this was quite an occasion, although I imagine they must have been taken out class by class, not all at one time. Exercise was important and, in the 1905 advertisement, we are told that an instructor in 'drilling' – physical exercises – was employed there. This would be where the pleasure grounds came in handy.

Before Mollie's time, there was a great happening written up in the local paper. The sleeping quarters were housed in Clevelands and Rosemont where the head mistress, Miss Wiltshier, had a sitting room, although the staff slept next door at Rycote

Lodge. One night as she was retiring, she accidentally kicked the gas tap with her foot, with the result that, when the maid came in the following morning with a lighted candle, there was a terrific blast. The maid was blown through the hall into and out of the drawing room, ending up in the garden in the rose bushes. Miraculously, she was only scratched! One of the girls was still asleep on the floor above while her bed just balanced on the edge of the large hole in the floor caused by the explosion. The room was called the Explosion Room for years afterwards.

Plate 23: The school following the explosion

In her book, Mollie includes a page of photographs which show the house when she was there, as well as Miss Wiltshier, who was nicknamed 'Dub-Dub' because she had a knack of knowing everything that went on, as though she could hear jungle drums.

One of Mollie's many escapades at the school was to disguise herself as a boy to go and buy ice creams on The Beach. She also took part in a school production of *The Beggar's Opera*, which became part of the life of the school for some time.

The school continued until 1935 when a Miss Pulham took

it over and moved to Hallam Road. It does not seem to have lasted for long afterwards. Miss Wiltshier died in Kent in 1937, having remained at the school until 1935. In 1937, the most recent Directory we have access to records the Misses Nichols living at Clevelands and the house has been a private residence ever since.

Chapter 9

Three born in Clevedon:
Jan Morris, Christopher Morris and Gareth Morris

Mr. and Mrs. Walter Morris, who lived in Clevedon during the 1920s and 1930s, produced three interesting sons. Two of them have written short pieces for me about their Clevedon childhoods. They follow this short introduction about their parents and their own careers.

Walter Morris died in 1938, having been gassed in the First World War, leaving his widow with their three sons to support. Enid Morris, née Payne, was the daughter of the manager of Lloyd's Bank in Monmouth where she met and married Walter Morris in 1919. In the 1891 Census, her father gave his occupation as 'bank cashier and Professor of Music'. Sadly, his musical talent was never fully realised and, in later census returns, he can be seen rising steadily to higher positions in banking.

Enid studied at the Conservatory in Leipzig under Teichmuller and was musically highly gifted. She and her husband were living in Clevedon in 1920 in a house called The Lookout on Marine Hill, later renting part of Grosvenor House in Victoria Road. A few years later, they moved to 1 Herbert Road and their three sons were born here: Gareth in 1920, Christopher in 1922 and James in 1926. They later lived at Verwood in Madeira Road.

Enid Morris was, at various times, the organist at St. John's Church in Clevedon and at St. Paul's at Walton in Gordano. This talented and well-qualified musician and teacher inaugurated the organ installed in January 1929 at the Picture House in Old Church Road by Percy Daniel's Organ Works, then based in East Clevedon. She was well known for her piano recitals in the early days of radio broadcasting in the West Country and South Wales.

Her oldest son, Gareth, wrote:

During my tenure as principal boat boy at St John's Church, Clevedon, Somerset, (c.1927-9) the organ there was blown by a water-powered engine. The organist at that time was my mother. A woman of devout beliefs, she was not blessed with any understanding of mechanical contrivances and at the elaborate ceremonial on the highest feast days was wont to pull out all the stops. The unfortunate engine in the bowels of the organ invariably succumbed at the loudest climax of my mother's triumphant performance; it had to be encouraged to renew its efforts by a churchwarden. During his descent through a trapdoor beneath the organ seat my mother could be heard apologizing: 'I am sorry; wretched thing; thank you so much!'

Gareth, the oldest son, became the finest flautist in Britain and played the flute in Westminster Abbey at the Coronation in 1953. He was Professor of Flute at the Royal Academy of Music from 1945 until 1985. For 24 years he was Principal Flautist with the Philharmonia Orchestra of London. He premiered works by composers such as Poulenc and Prokofiev, as well as adjudicating at prestigious competitions and sitting on various key committees for the Arts Council and the Incorporated Society of Musicians Soloists Section. His career was long and distinguished. He died in 2007.

The second son, Christopher, was also closely involved with music, both as a composer of some merit and as Musical Editor at the Oxford University Press. He trained as a chorister at Hereford Cathedral, training with Percy Hull as organist. He was a noted player of that instrument. After his war service he returned to his studies and attended the Royal Academy of Music. He joined

the Oxford University Press in 1954, eventually becoming head of music there. He developed the company's own record label.

He was instrumental in producing a new edition of *The Oxford Book of Carols*, enlisting help from Ralph Vaughan Williams and other leading modern composers.

Plate 24: Christopher Morris

Ten years after that, he selected the rising young composer John Rutter to work on a new collection. He also made arrangements of musical works for the organ and edited many collections of music.

As well as making immense efforts with the work of others, Christopher was himself an excellent composer for voices, having worked with choirs for many years. He also wrote well for piano. In 1985, he was elected a Fellow of the Royal Academy of Music. On his retirement the following year, he was awarded an honorary MA by the University of Oxford. He continued to play the organ in retirement. Christopher died in 2014.

Last but by no means least, we have James. James went into the 9th Royal Lancers and served during the Second World War. His career was in both journalism and literature and his travel writing led the field for many years. He married and had five children, losing one in infancy. He travelled widely, meeting Kim Philby, Che Guevara and Eisenhower. He also reported on Eichmann's trial in Jerusalem, visited Hiroshima following the nuclear bombing and was among the party which made the successful attempt on Everest in 1953.

Having felt for most of his life that he was in the wrong body, he progressed towards gender reassignment, becoming a woman in 1972. He wrote about this experience in *Conundrum*, which did much to help others in the same boat. Since then known as Jan, she has written altogether over 50 noted books, ranging from travel through politics and history to fiction.

Her three-volume history of the British Empire is a model work. In her travel books Jan's portrayal of great cities has been remarkable – those local people who have read her book on Venice have had the treat of seeing Kingston Seymour mentioned. Her vocabulary and subject matter is wide; at times, she travels her inner mind as well as writing about her own house in north Wales. She has a deep and abiding love for Wales and has written widely about that country. Venice, Sydney, Trieste, Hong Kong, South Africa, America, Canada – even Huddersfield in her story of the World Bank – and many more places have featured in Jan's piquant and racy prose.

We come full circle here to the oldest brother, Gareth. While he was playing for the Queen during the Coronation, James was reporting on the successful attempt on the summit of Everest. In many ways, his news – he was the first to report this great success to Britain – made the Coronation an even more remarkable event. What a coup for the family to have two such remarkable close links to the Coronation.

Here are the short reminiscences written for me, firstly by Gareth, lastly by Jan. Many thanks are due to them both.

Gareth Morris

I was born in a Nursing Home opposite St. Peter's Church in Clevedon. The house, no longer existing, is featured in a charming picture by a 19th century Lady Elton which hangs in our drawing-room; only the back of its handsome parapet can be seen in the foreground of the view of the coast in 1838, as she looked down admiringly at the promontory and ancient church of St. Andrew, with her easel on Dial Hill.

As small boys my brothers and I loved the town,

with its elegant Victorian pier to be enjoyed for a twopenny toll while consuming freshly baked buns, ships in the distance from far-away climes; and thrilling Campbells' steamers to take us on the high seas, where lurked terrifying monsters in the murky depths while we ate strawberries and cream in the grand dining room, near the powerful engines - and they could be stilled at a moment's notice by an order from the Captain on his bridge above.

Summers were long, hot and sunny. The holiday-makers arrived to stay in the Edwardian

 hotels and boarding houses, bringing children with buckets and spades for the sandless beaches and still the Clevedon residents, those old ladies, clergymen and retired colonels continued to take their daily constitutionals, thus preserving the standards of the local guide book, which

Plate 25: Gareth Morris informed its readers that 'Clevedon prides itself - and rightly too - on being that rare thing, a fashionable watering-place that has retained its individuality'.

Schools were irritants that interrupted those idyllic days; when sentenced at the age of 5 to incarceration in Miss Pulham's kindergarten, my considered opinion was that they should be condemned. After the delights of private instruction in reading and playing chess by our splendid great-aunt (born 1853) this was indeed a shock, and I did not recover until I had served a period at Mr Usher's St. Leonard's Preparatory School for Boys, and endured a spell at Bristol Cathedral School, whence I managed to extricate myself when I was sixteen.

It seemed that my brothers were content at their boarding schools, but at home in Somerset I discovered the flute, and found emancipation: I taught myself to play with such determination that lessons in London with the greatest player of the day were arranged, they took precedence of conventional education, and my own voracious reading confirmed that school was not for me. I departed for London, the magnet of my aspirations with its golden streets, but I owed a great deal to Clevedon and its surroundings, where I had gained enormous experience in numerous amateur orchestras in Bristol, Weston-super-Mare and with Clevedon's own Silver Band; as its youngest member and lone woodwind player I was given the warmest welcome, and a prominent position on the lovely bandstand in the sun.

After so many years in London it is a delight to return to the West Country, to enjoy the beautiful house we have found in Clifton - and discover that Clevedon has not lost its individual charm.

The nursing home where Gareth was born was Peterhurst. It stood on the corner of Alexandra Road and Copse Road, opposite St Peter's Church. Miss Pulham taught in a house in Albert Road. Mr Usher's school was at 16 Madeira Road.

Jan Morris

Such memories as do survive are entirely delightful - the sun shone every day, as I remember it! - and are almost entirely to do with the sea. In those pre-war days a marvelous stream of shipping constantly moved up and down the Bristol Channel, in and out of the coal ports on the Welsh shore, in and out of Bristol itself. It became my passion to observe their passages. My proudest possession was a telescope, and I took it with me on rambles all the way along the Clevedon coast, from the Pill at one end, (where I

 remember seeing one of the last Bristol Channel sailing smacks unload its cargo of gravel into horse-drawn wagons), to the Portishead coastguard at the other where ships had so

Plate 26: Jan Morris   often to wait for the tide before proceeding to Avonmouth or the Bristol city docks. I made careful records, with drawings, about the vessels I saw, and I have been permanently affected by these missions (for I took them with great seriousness). All my life I have loved to watch the ships go by. All my life I have loved being alone to pursue my craft, as I was in the sunshine then. And all my life I have been an observer, a recorder and a remembrancer. Also never to this day, wherever I am in this world, do I hear a skylark sing in a wide blue sky without thinking of those long ago brackeny grasslands above the Bristol Channel, between the Pill and Portishead.

Chapter 10

South of the River: a village within a town
a reminiscence by Derek B. Lilly,
illustrated largely with photographs by the late Tom Lilly

My father, Thomas Lilly, was born in Clevedon in 1882 and returned to the town in about 1914. In that year, he bought a grocery business from George Westcott, whose shop lay at the north end of Brighton Terrace in Kenn Road. He'd led a very varied life before that, working as a quarryman, before going with some of his cousins to Wales to mine coal at the Ferndale Pit in the Rhondda Valley. He married Bertha Gale, one of his many cousins, and started his married life as an insurance salesman. George Westcott's brother had married a cousin of my father's and that cousin let my father know that the business would be coming up for sale.

The shop stood by the Middle Yeo river and, as my father ran it for over 50 years, it became a local landmark. In fact, for many years, locals called the river, 'Lilly's River'!

The river formed a boundary dividing our part of Kenn Road, together with Treefield Road and Hillview Avenue, from the rest of the road. In those days, Clevedon was very much a town in which you identified with your own small locality. We always thought of ourselves as Kenn Roaders and did not associate with Stroud Roaders, having little to do with the folk who lived elsewhere.

A lot happened to our family in the early years of running the shop. When my parents moved there, they already had two children, Tom and Marianne. More followed soon after, Harry, Bert, Betty and last but not least, myself, completing the list in 1924 on New Year's Day. My mother died of meningitis in

September 1927 and Pa, as we always called my father, managed after that by drafting in help from outside to look after us children. The eldest, Tom, was seventeen, but I was only three so, while the older ones could cope pretty well, Olive Tossell looked after me for a while, followed by 'Aunt' Lizzie Mountstevens. Whether she was related or not, I haven't been able to find out, but plain and comfortable 'Aunt' fitted her well and we all enjoyed her company. When my brother Bert brought his young lady, Selma Johansen, to the house one Sunday, Aunt Lizzie was quite affronted to find that we'd given her bread and dripping for tea.

'Bread and dripping!' she said. 'When we've got company?'

Selma was very tickled to be thought of as company, being at the time only fifteen!

In 1927, when I was around three years old, a good way back now, we had a stump-tailed cat named Pete. As I was about all day we became great friends and, where I was, Pete was.

Plate 27: Derek Lilly with Pete the cat c1928

He was big, more like a small dog than a cat, and was content to sit on the doorstep of my father's shop in Kenn Road with me, watching out for the rare motorcar and the much more common milk cart.

Pete weighed in at around 10lbs and the only way I could carry him was to pick him up with my arms extended under his body and his legs hanging down on either side of my arms. This was quite all right with him and he stood patiently while I manoeuvred in order to do it. His mother, Judy, was an excellent ratter and would haunt the boundaries of Yeates' Pit, in one month killing 40 rats which she brought home for us, as cats do. Pete was idle as far as catching things went. He did once bring in a chicken's head wrapped up in paper and on another occasion a rabbit skin. He was a good companion though and until the time I started school we were always to be seen around together.

The field behind the shop was always called Yeates' Pitch to distinguish it from Pugh's Pitch, a small green patch between the two terraces on the east side of the road, which now form Kennaway Road. Immediately behind those two terraces was the field we called Pugh's Backs, where a local butcher had pasture ground. It was used as an unofficial playground where school children played when they were at home. They were very much aware of the need to vanish if the word was passed 'Butcher Pugh is coming down the road'. He didn't like kids in his field and would rant and rave, waving his walking stick at them as they vanished from the field!

Yeates' Pitch should by rights have been called Shopland's Pitch because it was the site of their brick and tile works that had been set up near the railway line that ran across the west side of the field. They had probably started the works to produce materials for their house-building programme that started about 1880 and carried on into the 1920s, although the brick yard was sold out in 1898 to the brickworks run by Colonel Keen in Stroud Road.

The old clay pit, still there, had filled with water, and we were always told as youngsters to keep away from it. Dreadful tales were told to us of monster eels that could bite and drag us into the water. As a result we stayed out of that corner of the field. I learned later that actually the son of Bill Ford the milkman who lived up the road had drowned in the pit one winter when skating on ice that was too thin. The story of large eels was true though they weren't as big as the ones we had been told about. Later on, the Council used the pit as a rubbish dump and many of the eels and fish died from contamination of the water. Fred Clark, seen holding one of the fresh water conger eels in the picture below, was a 'character'.

Plate 28: Fred Clark with eel, late 1920s

In the spring he always professed to have seen the swallows arrive earlier than anyone else. I expect that if you had told him you saw one flying around on 1 January he would state that he had seen one 'just before Christmas'.

Yeates' Pitch near the back of my father's shop was always a popular place in winter and summer for the numerous unemployed young men during the Depression years. With unemployment pay running at around 17/- per week (i.e. 85 pence), this left very little money after a single man had paid over his keep to his mother. So football and cricket were played on the Pitch in the appropriate seasons. In actual fact, if anyone was on the dole for very long, Mr. Bennett the manager of the Unemployment Exchange often cut the little they were getting to 15/- or even 12/6d. If you got a good amateur team together to play sports for nothing, it was a good way to pass the time and keep yourself active.

Plate 29: Yeates pitch, late 1920s

In 1929, when I was five years old, I passed the 'Labour' every school morning on my way to the 'Sawmills School' as we youngsters called St Andrew's Infants School in Old Street. This was the Labour Exchange, then at Adanac House, built in the 1850s by the Eltons as a lodging house for single men who'd come to work in the town. In later years it was an orphanage, training children who were often sent off to the colonies to work as servants. It was demolished when the Great Western Road was laid out in the 1980s.

Plate 30: Adanac House, now beneath Great Western Road

Most days there would be a queue of men standing on the path there and overflowing along the pavement as well. Forty or maybe fifty men could be waiting in hope of work. Once they had signed on, there was nothing left for them to do but fill the time until dinner was ready. Older ones perhaps had allotments where they could grow vegetables to help feed their families, while younger ones with little or no money filled the time as best they could.

If the tide was in during the summer months there was always swimming down at the river mouth at Clevedon Pill. Although the Marine Lake had opened in 1929, to bathe or swim there cost money the chaps didn't have. Once the clap-hatch was shut and the water accumulated on the seaward side of the wall there was ample depth. The town sewer discharged into the river there, but when the tide was high the clapper on that closed up as well so the water was not too highly contaminated. I don't think that anyone went down with typhoid fever or cholera even though there were quite a number swimming there.

Plate 31: Swimming at Clevedon Pill, late 1920s

Kenn Road in those days was a much quieter place as far as traffic was concerned. In these two pictures there is not a car or person to be seen. This was around 1928 before the council houses were built and only field hedges show in the distance, on the right in Plate 31.

Plate 32: Kenn Road looking north, late 1920s

Plate 33: Kenn Road looking south, late 1920s

In all likelihood, my father was the only person 'south of the river' to own a camera. He had not purchased one, but won it as a prize for selling their flour from one of the flour companies. It was a very large size, a *Kodak* taking a 122 roll film rather than the 120, producing negatives that were about 4 inches by 3 inches. As a result, on many occasions, he was asked by neighbours to take shots for family reasons. Only a couple of these negatives have survived.

Plate 34: Les Bray   *Plate 35: Reg Bryce*

Reg Brice, who lived further down in the terrace of cottages, and Les Bray, from the newly built council houses, obtained jobs at the Picture House – now the Curzon – and were photographed in their button boy outfits standing out at the back by our garden gate.

Another good source of free gifts was the wrappers on the packs of a dozen boxes of England's Glory matches. Where are those stout matches today? They've been replaced by imported matches so flimsy that they snap if we are clumsy when trying to strike them. It is likely that these wrappers provided my older brother Tom with his first camera and got him started on taking photographs of local kids holding their own 'carnival', chaps swimming at the Pill and the old football and cricket matches on Yeates' Pitch.

As a family, we were lucky because, as well as taking over George Westcott's shop, my father later purchased a travelling household supplies business from Mr Vincent who was giving up his shop in the Triangle. Later, when my brother Tom had left school, a Ford Model T Great War ex-ambulance was bought and Tom and my father started to expand the provisions round into the surrounding countryside. When Tom was old enough to drive, he took over the outside round with my brother Harry when he in turn left school.

Plate 36: Model T with Tom Lilly

Harry was a great leg-puller and joker. In the hot summers of the 30s, we bought a second-hand bell tent and, with permission from Jack Marshall of Wrangle Farm in Moor Lane, put it up in his orchard.

Plate 37: Bell tent

As soon as it arrived it was set up, during the school holidays, on Yeates' Pitch: they wanted to be certain that everything was OK with it before taking it over to Wrangle Farm.

Pestered by school kids asking what it was about, Harry said, 'We are putting it up for the circus'.

'Garn you can't have a circus in that, it's too small', was the retort.

'Don't be daft, of course you can't', Harry came back with. 'It is for the ring master to use as an office. He's got to have it set up before the circus comes in on the train.'

Now this was logical as far as the kids were concerned because, at that time, the circus would arrive by train and unload at the siding away from the platform. Normally they would unload into the station yard and then parade down Kenn Road – not to Yeates' Pitch where our tent was, but to the field at Pugh's Backs. That small technicality didn't occur to them, however. Off they all trooped up to the station where the more the porters told them there was no circus coming in, the more convinced they were that they were just being got out of the way. Meanwhile, the bell tent was erected and checked for fitness in peace and quiet.

The Middle Yeo had always played a great part in the life of us kids. In the winter we would be sliding along on the ice and in the summer there were tadpoles to catch and redbreasts and minnows, as well as 'loggers' as we called the occasional loaches that were unfortunate enough to come within our reach. When I was told my minnows had died, for years I accepted this. However, my sister Marianne would surreptitiously pour them back into the water while I was at school.

Plate 38: Weekly bonfire of rubbish

There was always a bonfire lit at least once a week because, in those days, there was no business rubbish collection. Cardboard boxes and paper that had accumulated were taken into Yeates' Pitch field and burned. During the school holidays, this was always a great attraction for us kids and we would gather round and watch, sometimes baking potatoes in the ashes filched from the allotments on the other side of the river. It was a simple matter of climbing over the back wall to get from the gardens of the two terraces into Yeates'.

In the thirties, food was at a premium for some families in Kenn Road. My brother Bert always used to say about one lad who was eating an apple, probably scrumped from a farm orchard, that when another boy asked, 'Can I have the core?' the reply was, 'There ain't gonna be no core'. Many years later, when Bert and his daughter were talking about this, he described the sheer poverty of those Depression years between the Wars, and told her that he'd seen kids pick up orange peel and eat it: they were that hungry, poor little devils.

We always used to say, 'You are never a real Kenn Roader unless you have fallen into the river.' I reckon I held the record for that: I fell in three times in one day when I was around six years old. In the summer the water levels always dropped, and this was the time for the bigger lads to create 'Bankers'. They would crumble dirt

Plate 39: Preparing to jump the Middle Yeo

from the stream bank to make a small platform and jump from one bank down onto the landing place. The other challenge was to jump the river from the bank by our oil-shed and land on the top of the bank on the other side. This was reasonably easy but woe betides you if you landed short. You did not drop into the river but into a bed of stinging nettles below the bank itself. There is a matronly lady who now lives at Pill who still reproaches me when we meet nowadays for egging her on to try the jump. Alas she failed and got herself stung. Worse still, if you let go of the nettles, you could topple backwards into the river itself.

The bank on the south side of the river was a few feet higher than the north. This was because of the 'slubbing' or cleaning out the bottom of the river that was done every few years. The official right of way ran along the north bank so the mud and plants removed from the river bed were always thrown onto the south bank. Over the years they made a difference of a few feet. By our sheds there was a concrete reinforcing wall to the bank which made a good take-off place with a 14- or 15-foot run and a good 2-foot drop to the other side. A little further down the river it was earth again and sloping rather more steeply. The garden fence at Yeeles' house left only about 10 feet to get a run.

There was one local boy who we will simply call Bill who always fell for a mug. When a crowd of them gathered and started bank jumping it was very easy and I started it off by saying, 'Well I never thought that I would see it but Kitey Powell jumped the bank up by Yeeles' fence.'

Bill straight away bristled up. 'He couldn't, it's too wide,' he said.

'Well if I hadn't seen it I wouldn't have believed it myself. You were there John weren't you?'

'Yes', came the reply, 'but of course Kitey could do it easily. I don't reckon anyone else could.'

That was like red rag to a bull. Bill straight away stalked up to where the supposed jump had taken place. A quick run and jump and Bill ended up in around one foot of mud and two feet of water.

A big advantage of Yeates' Pitch was that, as well as being useful for cricket games in the summer and football at almost any time of the year, it offered a good motorcycle circuit. All the boys in our family were bike addicts. I myself was not able to take full part pre-War and had to wait until 1947 when I was demobbed after five years in the army. However, my three older brothers all had motorcycles by 1938. In the early 30s, Harry had a very nice AJS side-valved-engine bike. It was unusual by today's standards because the control levers were backward working. The cables went through the handlebars and there was no twist-grip throttle control. The left hand used the clutch while the right hand had two levers, one for the front brake and the other for the petrol supply.

Plate 40: Marianne Lilly on the AJS motorbike

Came the day when Charlie Hale from across Kenn Road had his first riding lesson. It was explained to him that he was to drive from the bottom corner of the field along the rough path then turn left and go along the cart track. He should then follow the track around until he came to the other corner where he would turn left again and get back to where he has started. 'If you want to stop', he was told, 'pull the left-hand lever and the bottom lever on the right hand side.' He was not told about changing gear but was to drive slowly around in bottom gear on the hand gear change machine.

All began well. He went along nicely until he was approaching the river, then he forgot what to do and tugged on the throttle lever instead of the brake. Then, when he realised what was happening, he pulled in the clutch. The bike whizzed merrily up over the slight hump of the bank and Charlie finished down in the river with the bike, not merry at all. Needless to say he was covered with mud and soaked to the skin. The bike was pulled out and Charlie tottered across the road to change into dry clothes. Luckily for him his mother was out of the way in the back garden talking over the garden wall to the next door neighbour. Charlie sneaked in through the kitchen leaving a trail of mud and dirty water behind him.

He had not come back over to the shed for very long when his mother came to the front gate. She wasn't one to cause a scene.

'Charlie', she called out in honeyed tones, 'I want to see you a minute.'

'Yes Mother', called out Charlie in reply, 'I'll be over later on', and muttered 'A lot later on too.' Charlie never did learn either to ride a motorbike or drive a car.

'Before the War.' How often has that phrase run through my mind when I have been sorting through my memories? A great deal has changed in the years since those times. In pre-War years, refrigeration was seldom seen except maybe in butchers' shops. We used to get a delivery from the *Walls' Ice Cream* branch and it arrived via the railway goods delivery, in insulated boxes. They were chilled inside by the addition of 'dry ice'. This was carbon dioxide in solid form used as a freezing or chilling agent. It evaporated slowly leaving no moisture behind because it was a gas. It was very dangerous to leave it indoors because it could be lethal if it spread in a closed atmosphere. The ice cream rapidly sold out and the box of dry ice was generally taken up to the sheds where the frozen lump was tipped out on the river bank to evaporate in open air.

One day Harry idly kicked it into the river where it started bubbling as it slowly dissolved and sank in the mud at the bottom. Even with the warming effect of the river water it was still blowing bubbles a half hour afterwards. Harry wandered over to look every once in a while and, as he was doing so, a neighbour going home the short way to Hillview Avenue asked, 'What are you looking at in the river?'

Harry in perfect truth said, 'I've been watching those bubbles coming up through the mud'.

'It must be a gas leak,' said the man, 'someone should do something about it.'

Now how anyone could imagine that a gas pipe or main was laid in the bed of the river passes comprehension. In fact, the gas pipe was put across by the road bridge where it was in full view!

However, Harry, always on the lookout for a bit of fun, replied, 'Well I am keeping my eye on it to see if it gets worse'.

With that the man went on his way. Shortly after, he came back again with his wife and the next door neighbours. Believe it or not they stood watching for around 20 or 30 minutes until the dry ice had finally evaporated.

I often wonder how it happened that the services we had in the 1930s vanished so quickly after the war with the birth of the supermarket. Even in lower Kenn Road we had at that time four bakers who delivered daily as a matter of course. I remember even today with great delight what happened after one baker had called on a house with their bread order. Kemp's in Stroud Road used to deliver using a small Coburg cart driven by a lady called Beattie. She was always known as Beattie Kemp although that was not her surname.

At one call she was always invited in by the customer for a cup of tea and a chat about whatever had been happening locally. On this particular day the pony had dropped a desirable deposit in the road. In those days, with so many horses and carts travelling up and down Kenn Road, this occurred fairly regularly and the droppings were very soon collected up for gardens and allotments. Very useful stuff! As the Coburg went on to the next call, the woman living next to Beattie spotted it. She came out quickly with a bucket and coal shovel to collect it and set it around the roses bushes in her front garden.

This did not suit the woman who'd paid for the bread, who started shouting at her, 'You have no rights to do that. I am her customer and that was mine'.

The 'debate' with ever stronger language conducted at the two garden gates entertained a growing audience. Finally they realised they were 'on stage' as it were and disappeared back into their respective houses.

The grocers' shops in the Triangle area numbered nine, to my reckoning. We had at least six butchers in the lower town, most of them sending out to accept midweek orders and week end orders, and offering delivery.

Plate 41: Gould's Butcher's trap from Old Street shown here in the Tickenham Road

Farmers or small-holders came around with milk in cans, measuring out into jugs, pints or half pints. This happened wind or rain, snow or frost. Yet today we have to trudge up and down in all weathers to the local emporium that we favour with our business. Woe betides us if we inquire or ask for something not on the display shelves. 'There's no demand for it' we are told. What is truly meant is that the turnover for that particular product is not high enough to justify stocking it, or the profit margin on it is regarded as too small. Who are we as customers to question what we can buy? That seems to be the attitude today.

I look back at those pre-War years and remember that, while labourers finished their day's work at 5pm, shops stayed open until 7pm, 7.30pm Fridays, and 8pm Saturdays. My brothers, Tom and Harry, having come back from the oil round would still be working after tea up in the shed. The business in those days ordered everything in bulk so the grocer packed everything himself. There was washing soda to be weighed and bagged, our own Towel Soap to be wrapped up in the printed paper coupon, starch and borax to pack from the loose tubs, and the van to be loaded up with general stock and customers' orders ready for the following day.

The Primus pressure lantern gave a better light than the street lights and needless to say friends would gather round a bonfire of discarded packaging that was often lit on the bank of the river. Although some of their friends were working, money was not plentiful, and coming to have a sociable chat passed the time when you hadn't the money to go out to the pub or to the pictures.

When Tom was old enough to drive, he took over the outside round with my brother Harry who, by then, had left school. Around 1927-8, he was approached by a soap traveller for a firm in the Liverpool area. Lancashire was a hotbed of small soap-boiler firms. This firm had branched out and they made soap that was packed in cardboard packs with a coupon on it. After saving 20 coupons you could exchange them for a hand towel.

When we tried it out, it proved to be fairly popular with the customers and Tom had an idea. When the traveller came round the following month he asked what price the soap would be with our name imprinted on it, packed plain with no wrapping and without the towels. Towels to be ordered when wanted but not supplied in quantity. The traveller asked the firm about this and a successful agreement was reached.

So Tom had paper wrappers printed and worked out the number of wrappers to be exchanged for hardware items. A frying pan, for example, would be, say, 20 wrappers. It was possible to use them for any of the lines that we sold. Things like half tea services, saucepans, kettles or any of the goods sold on the hardware side. Coupons were valued at about a halfpenny each against the purchase. Pountney's potteries of Fishponds' Lodge Causeway made tea sets in the Thames Valley pattern that were very popular. Since we sold other items in that range, the customer could build up the set with dinner plates, teapots and so forth.

Tom's *Lilly's Towel Soap* business expanded until over half the washing soap being sold was our own brand. The traveller for Lever's was very surprised when sales of *Christopher Thomas' Puritan Soap* from the Broad Plain factory in Bristol and *Sunlight Soap* from Lord Leverhulme's Port Sunlight were halved due to this! The same happened with Thomas Hedleys' Newcastle *Fairy Soap* as well. Lever's' traveller bought a pound of our towel soap to have it tested for quality and was astounded to find out that it was being sold at 5½d a pound against their price of 6d.

Plate 42: Lilly's
soap wrapper

Tom then showed him four bars of soap that had been put on one side after *Towel Soap* had started. One bar each of *Towel Soap*, *Sunlight*, *Puritan* and *Fairy*. In six months, the soap had of course dried out a little. However, our Towel Soap still weighed 7½ ounces, while the others, *Puritan*, *Sunlight* and *Fairy* had all dropped to just above 7 ounces.

At that time there were no laundry powders, just washing soap and hard scrubbing. Few people in the south-west used a dolly, a small three-legged stool on a long handle, used to agitate the washing in a tub. Down here it was mostly scrubbing boards, many with slightly corrugated metal centres that were inclined to wear thin and possibly tear the clothes eventually. It was a brave pioneer who thought up the idea of using thick glass cast with a ripple in it instead of the ridged metal. It took a lot of persuading to get staunch traditional washerwomen to change over. Of course they had to be warned not to plunge a cold scrubbing board into the bath of hot water without warming the board up a bit!

Around the time of the infamous Valentine's Day Massacre in Chicago, there had been several complaints made and remarks passed in Town Council meetings about the conduct of some inhabitants in the newly built Hillview Avenue. Chatting was going on one evening around the bonfire behind the shop and a couple of friends came across to Harry who was busy weighing soda. They had a piece of broken wood from a soap box that was about to go on the fire. They asked if they could borrow a paint brush and have a dip of creosote. Painting the words Chicago Street on the wood they next borrowed the ladder that hung on the side of the van. The board was duly nailed around ten feet up on the lamp post at the top of Hillview Avenue where it stayed for several years.

One of the housewives was heard to complain to her next door neighbour: 'Fancy saying Chincango Street. We are not like that down here!'

By the spring of 1939 I was working at W.H. Hiatt's gents' outfitters shop in Old Street. As I was supposed to be learning the trade my wages were a princely 5/- (25p) per week. Commission was paid, sorted by a price ticket code, but, as I was second sales to Tom Garland, if I was lucky, my commission might get me 2/6 (12.5p) a month. Hours were from 9am until 1pm and then 2pm until 7pm, 7.30pm on Friday and 8pm on Saturday. I also had to go to Mr Hiatt's house at the top of Queen's Road and get the shop keys that were hanging on a hook inside the front door. That meant I had to be there by around 8.45am to get to the shop before 9am.

Plate 43: Hiatt's shop, 11 and 13 Old Street

In that summer Tom Garland was called up and, still on 5/- per week, I was left, to all intents and purposes, running the men's department by myself. At the start of the war, blackout was imposed and this meant going home in the pitch black when the shop shut at 7pm.

I can remember when the autumn sale was held that year, Mr Hiatt said to me at around 9.45pm on the last Saturday of the sale, 'We have not had a customer come in for five minutes or so, Lilly. You may as well lock the door and tidy up'.

It was nearly impossible to keep all the packets of winter vests and pants etc. all separated and, if I had tried to pack stuff away before seeing to the next customer, those waiting would have got annoyed. So that left a lot of tidying up still to do.

After a very quick packing up, Mr Hiatt grudgingly admitted that the shelves 'Would do for now, although if you wish to go on to Cole and Pottow as an "improver", you will have to do better than that'.

Because I could not get a battery for my bike lamp, I found myself walking home at around 10.15pm bumping into the occasional lamp post as I went down Kenn Road. However, I got an extra 5/- for that week, and my commission for the month was boosted – so it wasn't all bad.

I don't know whether some of my brother Harry's humour had rubbed off on me, but I recall once that I was standing at the front counter in the shop when a youngster came in with a note and some money.

The note asked for a reel of black cotton. 'Light or dark black?', I asked him.

'I'll find out', he said, and before I could stop him he was out of the shop. He returned a little later entering the ladies' side of the shop with another note.

This meant he saw Miss Coombs, the manageress, so she took me thoroughly to task. 'You are not here to poke fun at customers, Lilly', she told me, tartly. I am afraid that Kenn Road humour was permitted no existence in Old Street.

In 1940, after being there for 12 months, I had a pay rise to 7/6d. I was still running the men's side of the shop by myself, but when clothing coupons started it meant a reduction of purchases, and no more sales weeks.

On the first day of January in 1941, I was 17 years old, old enough to hold a driving licence. My father had been finding it more and more difficult to get a driver for the oil round so, in the summer, I told Mr Hiatt I was finishing. 'Going into munitions work I suppose?' he asked.

'No', I replied 'I am going to go driving for my father until I get called up.'

At last my dreams were fulfilled. Apart from five years of driving during my army service, I was driving on the oil round for 21 years and then on a milk round for another 21 years. I think that the spell playing about in the old Model T was what inspired me. I have never wanted to be anything during my working life, but a delivery man. Out in all winds and weathers but doing a job I enjoyed, with never a day on the 'dole' until I had to take early retirement at 64¼ in April 1988. However, later I still managed to get a part time job delivering that lasted until I finally gave up at the age of 83.

I had great enjoyment whilst working for *Horlick's Dairies* tormenting a fellow rounds-man. He was saying about how long he had been driving and I casually said, 'Well I was behind the wheel 50 years ago'.

He immediately bristled up and replied, 'Impossible'.

I said, 'Well I'll bring proof to work tomorrow'.

When I showed him this photo of a very small me sitting at the wheel of the old Model T, he said, 'You said you was driving 50 years back. You couldn't have driven then'.

Plate 44: Derek Lilly behind the wheel of the Model T Ford, c1926

I could not resist so I returned with 'Len, a good rounds-man takes in what is SAID, not what he thinks is said. I stated that I was behind the wheel, not that I had driven'.

Going back to the 30s, Saturday mornings were always to be looked forward to. For some of the lads whose family owned a pair of trucks there was money to be made. The gas works sold bags of coke for 6d per bag or two bags for 11d. Anyone with trucks large enough to carry two bags could make a penny each delivery. As well as that, they would maybe get a penny for fetching the coke or perhaps even, joy of joys, tuppence! My father would not allow me to do that because, as he said, 'There are other boys who need it a lot more than you do'.

I used to help Chick Youde a school friend, fetching his quota. On Friday after school he would go round to his usual customers and let them know he could collect their order. On Saturday he would be at their house sharp to collect the cash, then off up to the gas works in Moor Lane. There was normally a queue for the coke, but his father Charlie worked at the gas works, so Chick always used to get in quick. Back down the road as fast as we could, with one of us pulling on each handle of the old trucks. The iron wheels rumbling over the uneven road surface echoed as we went. Make the delivery and then over to the gas works again to collect for bags for the next pair of customers.

With luck he would make as much as 6d, or even 9d if he was lucky. He could get into the matinee Saturday afternoon for 4d sitting in the wooden 7d seats in the front row at the Picture House. If Doris was in the box there was never any problem about getting in whatever the film's rating was, but if it was Mrs Cox (stepmother of the owner, Victor Cox) she was a tartar as far as 'A' films were concerned. However if we were desperate to see it, we could always go to the other end and get a half price seat in the shillings.

In the summer months, a Saturday afternoon would see us kids sitting in rows along the wall above the river waiting patiently. What for? In those days few racing pigeon keepers could afford their own clock. Anyone living in Kenn road would have to 'clock-in' at *Hancock's Printing Works* near the top of Kenn Road. The distance from the cote to Hancock's clock had been measured and the time it should take to run between the two would be deducted from the clock. Therefore a speedy runner was a good bonus for an owner. Pigeons are seen in the sky – down they come – well-trained birds flew straight into the cote. The rubber racing ring removed from their legs into the runners hands. Out from the 'drumway', the alley between the blocks of houses, comes Kitey Brooks, Round from Pugh's Back comes Jerry Miles. Off they go up Kenn Road. Us kids sitting on the wall of the bridge were thrilled to death to watch the race. Olympics? HAH! We would sooner see Kenn Roaders running.

Plate 45: One of the boys taking pigeons to the station

In the lower part of Kenn Road, a little further toward Kenn Village than the thatched cottage, there was a large ash tree that overhung its branches across the road. Now remember that in those days street lighting was limited to lights that cast a circle around the lamp posts and little else. Moreover the lights ended near the telephone box that stands between 160 and 162. People were reliant on bicycles more than cars and the rather feeble bike lights were more to allow others to see that someone was coming rather than light the way of the cyclist.

All these factors led to the arrival of the Kenn Road

ghost. It was a simple matter for two of my older brothers and their friends to climb the ash tree and fasten a light rope to an overhanging branch. Measuring it off so that the loose end was around ten foot off the road surface, an old piece of white cloth and a weight was fastened to it. It was then a simple matter to hide in the hedge and hold one end of the rope. Then, as a cyclist approached, you'd give the weighted cloth a good swing across and a ghostly white shape fluttered ten feet above the road, before the rider got too close and could see what it was.

Someone in the field on the opposite side of the road would catch it and hold it from swinging back to hang over the road from the branch. Operated around closing time for the public houses this worked well. Until, one night, it was not given enough of a push and failed to reach the hedge on the other side. Unfortunately as well, it was not a man who had visited the pub and he was quite capable of rational thinking. He very quickly made for the field gate a few yards down the road and set off in pursuit. My two brothers, and a chap we will call Charlie, set off across the field to the fence by the train lines dodging through and up the lines avoiding being caught by a whisker.

They arrived in the house with Charlie and I had the fright of my life. Running through the wire fence he had caught himself on the barbed wire and ripped across his nose and upper cheek and there was blood pouring down his face. It gave me a horror of barbed wire that's lasted the rest of my life. He was doctored up to stop the bleeding by my father, but had to go up to the hospital for stitches and bore the scars for the rest of his life. After that episode my father put a stop to any 'ghosting' forthwith.

In 1967 the lease ran out on the shop and terrace of cottages, and the property, which had been built cheaply, was in a very poor state. The previous lease owners had some years earlier sold to the Council. The terrace of cottages below ours had already been demolished and the site sold to a petrol company. Our family business closed after having been there for more than fifty years.

As I said before, I continued as a delivery man, working for *Horlick's Dairies* until I took early retirement. A few years later the Council built ten flats where the original Brighton Terrace had stood. When the 'shop row' was demolished, I was re-housed temporarily in Marson Road. However, when the opportunity came to have one of the flats, I accepted with alacrity. As far as I am concerned, 'Once a Kenn Roader, Always a Kenn Roader!' So here I am now, living about 50 feet away from the place where I was born in 1924.

In 1974 the Middle Yeo was culverted. 'Lilly's River' had gone underground and 'Middle Path' took its place. The old world of 'South of the River' vanished and the old Kenn Road finally ceased to exist.

www.clevedoncommunitybookshop.coop